ANTI-INFLAMMATORY DIET COOKBOOK

200 TASTY, HEALTHY RECIPES AND 6 SIMPLE WEEKLY MEAL PREP PLANS TO FIGHT INFLAMMATION AND IMPROVE YOUR IMMUNE SYSTEM

Eva Moore

Table of Contents

Introduction

An anti-inflammatory diet is a diet that reduces the body's inflammatory responses. In other words, food that is healthy for inflammation and those foods you should avoid on an anti-inflammatory diet.

This is a type of diet that has been gaining attention in recent years. This diet focuses on foods to help reduce inflammation, which are rich in omega-3 fatty acids and antioxidants.

Inflammation, which occurs when your body's immune response comes into contact with an irritant, can occur throughout the body.

Benefits of Inflammatory Diet

The main purpose of this diet is that it helps you achieve superior health by reducing inflammation. By eating less of foods that cause inflammation, such as trans fats, you can help reduce many risk for your health and gain more energy.

What to Eat?

On this diet, you should eat lots of omega-3 fatty acids. These foods are rich in the fatty acid called alpha-linolenic acid (ALA), an essential nutrient.

Experts recommend eating 1-2 tablespoons of flaxseed oil per day to get all the essential fatty acids you need. The recommended foods for the anti-inflammatory diet contain omega-3 fatty acids and antioxidants, such as fruits (especially blueberries and melons), vegetables (including cruciferous vegetables such as broccoli, cabbage, and kale), whole grains, nuts, seeds, and beans.

Foods to Avoid?

Avoid foods that rich in trans fats and saturated fats such as hydrogenated oils, margarine, shortening, and lard. Also, avoid foods made with refined sugars such as white bread, white rice, and processed snacks.

Also, you should avoid eating too much processed foods. These include pastries, baked goods (such as cookies), fried foods (such as French fries), and sugary beverages such as soda. Also, avoid alcoholic drinks.

How to Start?

First of all, you must cleanse your body by eliminating all processed foods from your diet. Then take a food inventory of what you eat for a week or even longer. This will help you found out which foods are suitable for this diet. Then you can start your anti-inflammatory diet plan. Make sure you include the right foods in your diet. Remember to take essential fatty acids to ensure that you get enough of them in your body. Some anti-inflammatory diets may include one-day fasts once or twice a week, but it is not recommended to do a complete fast. It is best to use this diet in your everyday life, and you'll soon see the results.

How to maintain the diet?

Some experts recommend ordering a balanced diet to keep you on this diet. You should also make sure you intake enough nutrients such as iron, calcium, vitamin D, and calcium.

You will also need to drink plenty of water so that your body can flush out all the toxins in it. You may also need to take regular exercise or at least some light exercise.

Chapter 1. Breakfast

1. Spinach Frittata

Preparation time: 10 minutes
Cooking time: 12 minutes
Servings: 2
Ingredients

- 2 cups of baby spinach
- 1 teaspoon of garlic powder
- 2 tablespoons of extra-virgin olive oil
- 8 beaten eggs
- 1/2 teaspoon of sea salt
- 2 tablespoons of grated parmesan cheese
- 1/8 teaspoon black pepper

Directions:

1. Preheat the broiler to the highest setting.
2. Warmth the olive oil in a big ovenproof skillet or pan (well-seasoned cast iron fits well) over medium-high heat until it starts shimmering.
3. Cook, stirring regularly, for around 3 minutes after introducing the spinach.
4. Whisk together the eggs, salt, garlic powder, and pepper in a medium mixing cup. Carefully spill the egg mixture over the spinach and cook for 3 minutes, or until the edges of the eggs begin to set.
5. Gently raise the eggs away from the pan's sides with a rubber spatula. Enable the uncooked egg to flow into the pan's edges by tilting it. Cook for another 2 or 3 minutes, just until the sides are solid.
6. Place the pan under the broiler and cover with the Parmesan cheese. Preheat the oven to broil for around 3 minutes, or before the top puffs up.
7. To eat, break into wedges.

Nutrition:
Calories: 203
Total Fat: 17g
Total Carbs: 2g
Sugar: 1g
Fiber: 1g
Protein: 13g
Sodium: 402mg

2. Mushroom and Bell Pepper Omelet

Preparation time: 10 minutes
Cooking time: 10 minutes
Servings: 2
Ingredients

- 1 sliced red bell pepper
- 6 beaten eggs
- 1/8 teaspoon ground black pepper
- 2 tablespoons of extra virgin olive oil
- 1 cup of sliced mushrooms
- 1/2 a teaspoon of sea salt

Directions:

1. Warmth the olive oil in a broad non-stick pan over medium heat until it shimmers.
2. Combine the mushrooms and red bell pepper in a mixing dish. Cook, stirring regularly, for around 4 minutes, or until tender.
3. Whisk together the salt, eggs, and pepper in a medium mixing cup. Set the eggs over the

vegetables and cook for around 3 minutes, or until the edges of the eggs begin to set.

4. Gently raise the eggs away from the pan's sides with a rubber spatula. Allow the uncooked egg to flow to the pan's edges by tilting it. Cook for 2 to 5 minutes until the edges and core of the eggs are set.

5. Set the omelet in half with a spatula. To eat, break into wedges.

Nutrition:
Calories: 336
Total Fat: 27g
Total Carbs: 7g
Sugar: 5g
Fiber: 1g
Protein: 18g
Sodium: 656mg

3. Yogurt, Berry, and Walnut Parfait

Preparation time: 10 minutes
Cooking time: 0 minutes
Servings: 2
Ingredients

- 2 tablespoons of honey
- 2 cups of Plain unsweetened coconut yogurt or plain unsweetened yogurt or almond yogurt
- 1 cup of fresh blueberries
- 1/2 cup of walnut pieces
- 1 cup of fresh raspberries

Directions:

1. Stir the yogurt and honey together. Divide into two bowls
2. Sprinkle in blueberries and raspberries along with A quarter cup of chopped walnuts

Nutrition:
Calories: 505
Total Fat: 22g
Total Carbs: 56g
Sugar: 45g
Fiber: 8g
Protein: 23g
Sodium: 174mg

4. Oatmeal and Cinnamon with Dried Cranberries

Preparation time: 5 minutes
Cooking time-8 minutes
Servings: 2
Ingredients

- 1 cup of almond milk
- 1 cup of oats
- 1 teaspoon of ground cinnamon
- 1 cup of water
- 1 pinch of sea salt
- 1/2 cup of dried cranberries

Directions

1. Get the almond milk, salt, and water to a boil in a medium saucepan.
2. Stir in the cranberries, oats, and cinnamon. Reduce the heat and stir for 5 minutes.
3. Remove the oats from heat. Allow the pot to stand for 3 minutes. Mix before serving.

Nutrition:
Calories: 101
Total Fat: 2g
Total Carbs: 18g
Sugar: 1g
Fiber: 4g
Protein: 3g
Sodium: 126mg

5. Green Tea and Ginger Shake

Preparation time: 5 minutes
Cooking time-0 minutes
Servings: 2
Ingredients

- 2 tablespoons of honey
- 2 tablespoons of grated ginger
- 2 tablespoons of matcha (green tea) powder
- 2 cups of skim milk
- 2 scoops of Low-fat Vanilla ice cream

Directions:

1. In a blender, merge all the ingredients and blend until smooth.

Nutrition:
Calories: 340
Total Fat: 7g
Total Carbs: 56g
Sugar: 50g
Fiber: 2g
Protein: 11g
Sodium: 186mg

6. Smoked Salmon Scrambled Eggs

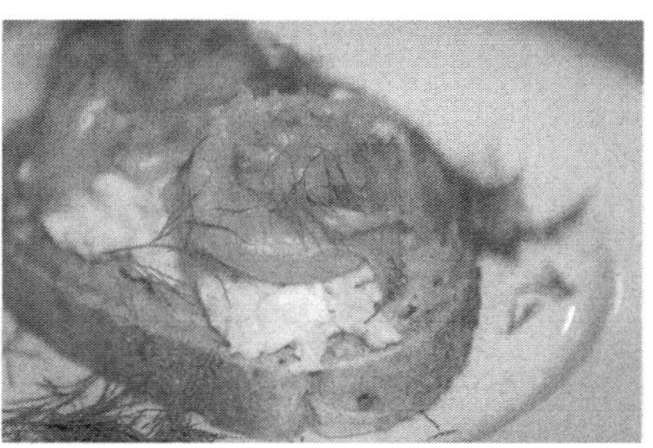

Preparation time: 5 minutes
Cooking time-8 minutes
Servings: 2
Ingredients

- 3 ounces of flaked smoked salmon
- 1/2 teaspoon of freshly ground black pepper
- 3/4 tablespoon of extra-virgin olive oil
- 4 beaten eggs

Directions:

1. Warmth the olive oil in a skillet or pan over medium-high heat until it starts shimmering.
2. Cook for around 3 minutes, stirring occasionally.
3. Set the eggs and pepper together in a medium mixing cup. Add them to the skillet or pan and cook, stirring gently, for around 5 minutes, or until cooked.

Nutrition:
Calories: 236
Total Fat: 18g
Total Carbs: 1g
Sugar: 1g
Fiber: 0g
Protein: 19g
Sodium: 974mg

7. Chia Breakfast Pudding

Preparation time: 10 minutes
Cooking time: 25 minutes
Servings: 2
Ingredients

- 1/2 cup of chia seeds
- 1/2 teaspoon of vanilla extract
- 1/2 cup of chopped cashews, divided
- 1 cup of almond milk
- 1/4 cup of maple syrup or honey
- 1/2 cup of frozen no-added-sugar pitted cherries, thawed, juice reserved, divided

Directions:

1. Combine the chia seeds, almond milk, maple syrup, and vanilla in a quart container with a tight-fitting seal. Set aside after thoroughly shaking.
2. Pour the pudding into two bowls and finish with a quarter cup of cherries and two tablespoons of cashews in each.

Nutrition:
Calories: 272
Total Fat: 14g
Total Carbohydrates: 38g
Sugar: 25g
Fiber: 6g
Protein: 7g
Sodium: 84mg

8. Coconut Rice with Berries

Preparation time: 10 minutes
Cooking time: 30 minutes
Servings: 2
Ingredients

- 3/4 cup of water
- 3/4 teaspoon of salt
- 1/2 cup of fresh blueberries, or raspberries, divided
- 1/2 cup of shaved coconut, divided
- 1/2 cup of brown basmati rice
- 1/2 cup of coconut milk
- 2 pitted and chopped dates
- 1/4 cup of toasted slivered almonds, divided

Directions:

1. Combine the water, basmati rice, coconut milk, spice, and date pieces in a medium saucepan over high heat.
2. Stir constantly until the mixture boils. Set the heat to low and cook, occasionally stirring, for 20 to 30 minutes, or until the rice is tender.
3. Place some blueberries, almonds, and coconut on top of each serving of rice.

Nutrition:
Calories: 281
Total Fat: 8g
Total Carbohydrates: 49g
Sugar: 7g
Fiber: 5g
Protein: 6g
Sodium: 623mg

9. Overnight Muesli

Preparation time: 10 minutes
Cook time-0 minutes
Servings: 2
Ingredients

- 1 cup of gluten-free rolled oats
- 1 cup of coconut milk
- 1/4 cup of no-added-sugar apple juice
- 1 tablespoon of apple cider vinegar (optional)
- 1/2 cored and chopped apple
- Dash ground cinnamon

Directions:

1. Combine the oats, apple juice, coconut milk, and vinegar in a medium mixing dish.
2. Refrigerate overnight, covered.
3. The following day, add the sliced apple and a pinch of cinnamon to the muesli.

Nutrition:
Calories: 213
Total Fat: 4g
Total Carbohydrates: 39g
Sugar: 10g
Fiber: 6g
Protein: 6g
Sodium: 74mg

10. Spicy Quinoa

Preparation time: 10 minutes
Cooking time: 20 minutes
Servings: 2
Ingredients

- 1 cup of water
- 1/4 cup of hemp seeds
- 1/2 teaspoon of ground cinnamon
- Pinch salt
- 1/4 cup of chopped hazelnuts
- 1/2 cup of quinoa rinsed well
- 1/4 cup of shredded coconut
- 1 tablespoon of flaxseed
- 1/2 teaspoon of vanilla extract
- 1/2 cup of fresh berries of your choice, divided

Directions

1. Combine the quinoa and water in a medium saucepan over high heat.
2. Set to a boil, then lower to low heat and continue to cook for 15 to 20 minutes until the quinoa is tender.
3. Combine the coconut, flaxseed, hemp seeds, cinnamon, vanilla, and salt in a large mixing bowl.
4. Divide the quinoa into two bowls and finish with some berries and hazelnuts for each serving.

Nutrition:
Calories: 286
Total Fat: 13g
Total Carbohydrates: 32g
Sugar: 1g
Fiber: 6g

Protein: 10g
Sodium: 44mg

11. Buckwheat Crêpes with Berries

Preparation time: 15 minutes
Cooking time: 5 minutes per crepe
Servings: 2
Ingredients

- 1/2 teaspoon of salt
- 1 cup of almond milk or water
- 1/2 teaspoon of vanilla extract
- 3 tablespoons of Chia Jam
- 1/2 cup of buckwheat flour
- 1 tablespoon of coconut oil (Half tablespoon melted)
- 1 egg
- 2 cups of fresh berries, divided

Directions:

1. Whisk together the salt, egg, buckwheat flour, and half tablespoon melted coconut oil, almond milk, and vanilla in a small mixing bowl until smooth.
2. Melt the remaining half tablespoon of coconut oil in a wide (12-inch) non-stick skillet or pan over medium-high heat. Tilt the pan to adequately cover it in the molten oil.
3. Using a ladle in the skillet or pan, pour half a cup of batter. Tilt the pan to properly brush it with batter.
4. Cook for another 2 minutes until the edges start to curl. Flip the crêpe with a spatula and cook for 1 minute on the other hand. Place the crêpe on a plate and set aside.
5. For the left batter, continue to make crêpe.
6. On a dish, place one crêpe, some berries, and a tablespoon of Chia Jam. Fold the crêpe over the filling and seal the edges.

Nutrition:
Calories: 242
Total Fat: 11g
Total Carbohydrates: 33g
Sugar: 9g
Fiber: 6g
Protein: 7g
Sodium: 371mg

12. Warm Chia-Berry Non-dairy Yogurt

Preparation time: 10 minutes
Cooking time-5 minutes
Servings: 2
Ingredients

- 1 tablespoon of maple syrup
- 1/2 vanilla bean halved lengthwise
- 2 cups of unsweetened almond yogurt or coconut yogurt
- 1 (10-ounce) package frozen mixed berries, thawed
- 1 tablespoon of freshly squeezed lemon juice
- 1/2 tablespoon of chia seeds

Directions:

1. Combine the berries, lemon juice, maple syrup, and vanilla bean in a medium saucepan over medium-high flame.
2. Get the mixture to a boil, continuously stirring. Reduce the heat to low heat and continue to cook for 3 minutes.
3. Switch off the heat from the pan. Detach the vanilla bean from the mixture and discard it. Add the chia seeds and mix well. Allow 5 to 10 minutes for the seeds to thicken.
4. Cover each bowl with one cup of yogurt and divide the fruit mixture among both of them.

Nutrition:
Calories: 246
Total Fat: 10g
Total Carbohydrates: 35g
Sugar: 21g
Fiber: 5g
Protein: 5g
Sodium: 2mg

13. Buckwheat Waffles

Preparation time: 15 minutes
Cooking time-6 minutes per waffle
Servings: 2
Ingredients

- 1/2 cup of brown rice flour
- 1/2 teaspoon of baking soda
- 1 egg
- 1 cup of buckwheat flour
- 1 teaspoon of baking powder
- 1/2 teaspoon of salt
- 1 tablespoon of maple syrup
- 1/2 cup of water
- 1 cup of almond milk
- Coconut oil for the waffle iron
- 1 teaspoon of vanilla extract

Directions:

1. Whisk together the buckwheat flour, baking powder, rice flour, baking soda, and salt in a medium mixing dish.
2. Add the maple syrup, egg, and vanilla to the dry ingredients. Whisk in the water and almond milk in a slow, steady stream until smooth.
3. The batter is absolutely free of lumps.
4. Allow 10 minutes for the batter to thicken slightly.
5. When the buckwheat is resting, it can settle to the bottom of the dish, so stir thoroughly before using.
6. Garnish the waffle iron with coconut oil and heat it.
7. In the waffle iron, pour the batter and cook according to the manufacturer's instructions.

Nutrition
Calories: 282
Total Fat: 4g
Total Carbohydrates: 55g
Sugar: 7g
Fiber: 6g
Protein: 9g
Sodium: 692mg

14. Coconut Pancakes

Preparation time: 10 minutes
Cooking time: 5 minutes per pancake
Servings: 2
Ingredients

- 1/2 cup of coconut, plus additional as needed
- 1/2 tablespoon of maple syrup
- 1/4 cup of coconut flour
- 1/2 teaspoon of salt
- 2 eggs
- 1/2 tablespoon of coconut oil or almond butter, plus additional for greasing the pan
- 1/2 teaspoon of vanilla extract
- 1/2 teaspoon of baking soda

Directions:

1. Using an electric mixer, combine the coconut milk, maple syrup, eggs, coconut oil, and vanilla in a medium mixing cup.
2. Combine the baking soda, coconut flour, and salt in a shallow mixing bowl. Set the dry ingredients with the wet ingredients in a mixing bowl and beat until smooth and lump-free.
3. If the batter is too dense, add more liquid to thin it down to a typical pancake batter consistency.
4. Using coconut oil, lightly grease a big skillet or pan. Preheat the oven to medium-high.
5. Cook until golden brown on the rim. Cook for another 2 minutes.
6. Continue to cook the leftover batter while stacking the pancake on a tray.

Nutrition:
Calories: 193
Total Fat: 11g
Total Carbohydrates: 15g
Sugar: 6g
Fiber: 6g
Protein: 9g
Sodium: 737mg

15. Spinach Muffins

Preparation time-15 minutes
Cooking time-15 minutes
Servings: 6
Ingredients

- 1 cup of packed spinach
- 1/4 cup of raw honey
- 1/2 teaspoon of vanilla extract
- 1/2 cup of almond flour
- 1/2 teaspoon of baking soda
- Pinch freshly ground black pepper
- Cooking spray
- 1 egg
- 2 tablespoons of extra-virgin olive oil
- 1/2 cup of oat flour
- 1 teaspoon of baking powder
- A pinch of salt

Directions:

1. Preheat the oven to 350 Fahrenheit.
2. Six muffin cups should be lined or greased with cooking oil.
3. Combine the olive oil, spinach, honey, eggs, and vanilla in a food processor. Blend until entirely smooth.
4. Set together the oat flour, almond flour, salt, baking soda, baking powder, and pepper in a medium mixing dish. Mix the spinach mixture well in the mixing cup.
5. Fill each muffin cup 2/3rd of the way with batter. Set the muffins in the oven for around 15 minutes or until gently browned and solid to the touch in the middle.
6. Detach the muffins from the pan and place them on a cooling rack to cool for 10 minutes before removing them.

Nutrition:
Calories: 108
Total Fat: 6g
Total Carbohydrates: 12g
Sugar: 6g
Fiber: 1g
Protein: 3g
Sodium: 217mg

16. Choco Chia Banana Bowl

Preparation time: 4 hours, 5 minutes
Cooking time: 0 minutes
Servings: 3
Ingredients:

- 1/2 -cup chia seeds
- 1-pc large banana, very ripe
- 1/2-tsp pure vanilla extract
- 2-cups almond milk, unsweetened
- 1-Tbsp cacao powder
- 2-Tbsps raw honey or maple syrup
- 2-Tbsps cacao nibs
- 2-Tbsps chocolate chips
- 1-pc large banana, sliced

Directions:

1. Combine the chia seeds and banana in a mixing bowl. By using a fork, mash the banana and mix well until thoroughly combined. Pour in the

vanilla and almond milk. Whisk until no more lumps appear.

2. Set half of the mix into a glass container, and cover it. Add the cacao and syrup to the remaining half mixture in the bowl. Mix well until incorporated. Pour this mixture into another glass container, and cover it. Refrigerate overnight both containers, or for at least 4 hours.

3. To serve, layer the chilled chia puddings equally in three serving bowls. Alternate the layers with the ingredients for mixing-in.

Nutrition:
Calories: 293
Fat: 9.7g
Protein: 14.6g
Sodium: 35mg
Total Carbs: 43.1g
Net Carbs: 36.6g

17. Blueberry Breakfast Blend

Preparation time: 8 minutes
Cooking time: 0 minutes
Servings: 1
Ingredients:

- 1/3-tsp turmeric
- 1/2-cup spinach
- 3/4 -cup fresh blueberries
- 1-cup fresh pineapple chunks
- 1-cup water
- 1-Tbsp chia seeds
- 1-Tbsp lemon juice

Directions:

1. Combine all the ingredients in your blender. Blend to a smooth consistency.

Nutrition
Calories: 260
Fat: 8.6g
Protein: 13g
Sodium: 30mg
Total Carbs: 39.5g

18. Quick Quinoa with Cinnamon and Chia

Preparation time: 15 minutes
Cooking time: 3 minutes
Servings: 2
Ingredients:

- 2-cups quinoa, pre-cooked
- 1-cup cashew milk
- 1/2-tsp ground cinnamon
- 1-cup fresh blueberries
- 1/4 -cup walnuts, toasted
- 2-tsps raw honey
- 1-Tbsp chia seeds

Directions:

1. In a saucepan, add the quinoa and cashew milk. Stir in the cinnamon, blueberries, and walnuts. Cook slowly for three minutes.

2. Remove the pan from the heat. Stir in the honey. Garnish with chia seeds on top before serving.

Nutrition:
Calories: 887
Fat: 29.5g
Protein: 44.3g
Sodium: 85mg
Total Carbs: 129.3g
Net Carbs: 110.8g

19. Plum, Pear and Berry-Baked Brown Rice Recipe

Preparation time: 12 minutes
Cooking time: 30 minutes
Servings: 2
Ingredients:

- 1-cup water
- 1/2-cup brown rice
- A pinch of cinnamon
- 1/2-tsp pure vanilla extract
- 2-Tbsps pure maple syrup (divided)
- Sliced fruits: berries, pears, or plums
- A pinch of salt (optional)

Directions:
1. Preheat your oven at 400F.
2. Bring the water and brown rice mixture to a boil in a pot placed over medium-high heat. Stir in the cinnamon and vanilla extract. Reduce the heat to medium-low. Simmer for 18 minutes, or until the brown rice is tender.
3. Fill two oven-safe bowls with equal portions of the rice. Pour a tablespoon of maple syrup into each bowl. Top the bowls with the sliced fruits and sprinkle over a pinch of salt.
4. Put the bowls in the oven. Bake for 12 minutes, or until the fruits start caramelizing and the syrup begins bubbling.

Nutrition:
Calories: 227
Fat: 6.3g
Protein: 14.1g
Sodium: 80mg
Total Carbs: 32.2g

20. Good Grains with Cranberries and Cinnamon

Preparation time: 8 minutes
Cooking time: 35 minutes
Servings: 2
Ingredients:

- 1-cup of grains (choice of amaranth, buckwheat, or quinoa)
- 21/2-cups coconut water or almond milk
- 1-stick cinnamon
- 2-pcs whole cloves
- 1-pc star anise pod (optional)
- Fresh fruit: apples, blackberries, cranberries, pears, or persimmons
- Maple syrup (optional)

Directions:
1. Bring the grains, coconut water, and spices to a boil in a covered saucepan. Reduce the heat to medium-low. Simmer until the grains are tender.
2. To serve, discard the spices and top with fruit slices. If desired, drizzle with the maple syrup.

Nutrition:
Calories: 628
Fat: 20.9g
Protein: 31.4g
Sodium: 96mg
Total Carbs: 112.3g

21. Seared Syrupy Sage Pork Patties

Preparation time: 12 minutes
Cooking time: 10 minutes
Servings: 2
Ingredients:

- 2-lbs ground pork, pastured
- 3-Tbsps maple syrup, grade B
- 3-Tbsps minced fresh sage
- 3/4-tsp sea salt
- 1/2-tsp garlic powder
- 1-tsp solid cooking fat

Directions:
1. Break the ground pork into chunks in a mixing bowl. Drizzle evenly with the maple syrup. Sprinkle with the spices. Mix well until thoroughly combined. Form the mixture into eight patties. Set aside.
2. Heat the fat in a cast-iron skillet placed over medium heat. Cook the patties for 10 minutes on each side, or until browned.

Nutrition:
Calories: 405
Fat: 11.2g

Protein: 30.3g
Sodium: 240mg
Total Carbs: 53.3g

22. Waffles Whipped With Perfect Plantain Pair

Preparation time: 12 minutes
Cooking time: 10 minutes
Servings: 2
Ingredients:

- 2-cups large plantains, medium-ripe, peeled and sliced
- 21/2-Tbsps coconut oil, melted
- 1-tsp apple cider vinegar
- 1-tsp pure vanilla extract
- 1-tsp cinnamon
- 1/2-tsp baking soda
- 1/2-tsp sea salt
- Choice of fresh fruit, maple syrup, and whipped coconut cream for serving

Directions:

1. Preheat your waffle iron to level 5 on its dial.
2. Combine the plantain and oil in your blender. Puree to a smooth consistency. Add the apple cider vinegar, vanilla, and cinnamon. Blend again on high speed until thoroughly combined. Add the baking soda and salt. By using a spatula, stir the mixture until forming a batter. Set aside.
3. Grease your waffle iron and pour 1/3 cup of the batter. Cook until the waffle turns brown to your liking.
4. Repeat until forming the batter. Ensure to grease the iron before pouring the batter. Stack the cooked waffles on a wire rack.
5. To serve, top each waffle with fresh fruit of your choice. Drizzle with the syrup, and then, garnish with the whipped coconut cream.

Nutrition:
Calories: 805
Fat: 26.8g
Protein: 40.2g
Sodium: 478mg
Total Carbs: 108.6g

23. Turkey with Thyme and Sage Sausage

Preparation time: 40 minutes
Cooking time: 25 minutes
Servings: 4
Ingredients:

- 1-lb ground turkey
- 1/2-tsp cinnamon
- 1/2-tsp garlic powder
- 1-tsp fresh rosemary
- 1-tsp fresh thyme
- 1-tsp sea salt
- 2-tsps fresh sage
- 2-Tbsps coconut oil

Directions:

1. Stir in all the ingredients, except for the oil, in a mixing bowl. Refrigerate overnight, or for 30 minutes.
2. Pour the oil into the mixture. Form the mixture into four patties.
3. In a lightly greased skillet placed over medium heat, cook the patties for 5 minutes on each side, or until their middle portions are no longer pink. You can also cook them by baking in the oven for 25 minutes at 400F.

Nutrition:
Calories: 284
Fat: 9.4g
Protein: 14.2g
Sodium: 290mg
Total Carbs: 36.9g

24. Sweet and Savory Breakfast Hash

Preparation time: 10 minutes
Cooking time: 15 minutes
Servings: 2
Ingredients:
For the turkey:

- 1/4 tsp. cinnamon
- 1/4 tsp. thyme (dried)
- 1/2 tbsp. coconut oil
- 1/2 lb. ground turkey
- Sea salt

For the hash:

- 1/4 tsp. garlic powder
- 1/4 tsp. thyme (dried)
- 1/4 tsp. turmeric
- 1/3 tsp. ginger (powdered)
- 1/2 tsp. cinnamon
- 1/2 tbsp. coconut oil
- 1/4 cup of carrots (shredded)
- 1 cup of butternut squash (cubed, you can also use sweet potato)
- 1 cup of spinach (you can also use other types of greens)
- 1/2 onion (chopped)
- 1 small apple (peeled, cored, chopped)
- 1 small zucchini (chopped)
- Sea salt

Directions:

1. In a skillet, heat half of the coconut oil over medium-high heat.
2. Add the turkey and cook until it's browned.
3. While cooking, season the meat with the spices and mix well.
4. Once cooked, move the turkey onto a plate.
5. Attach the remaining coconut oil into the skillet, along with the onion.
6. Sauté the onion until softened for about 2 to 3 minutes.
7. Add the apple, carrots, squash, and zucchini and cook until softened for about 4 to 5 minutes.
8. Attach the spinach and continue cooking until the leaves wilt.
9. Add the cooked turkey, along with the hash seasonings, and then continue mixing. Taste the hash and adjust the seasonings according to your taste.
10. Spoon the hash onto plates and serve.

Nutrition:
Calories: 1284
Fat: 103.02g,
Protein: 62.02g
Sodium: 184mg
Total Carbs: 28.23g

25. Five-Minute Avocado Toast

Preparation time: 5 minutes
Cooking time: 0 minutes
Servings: 1
Ingredients:

- 1/2 tsp. lemon juice (freshly squeezed)
- 1 tbsp. celery (chopped)
- 1/4 avocado
- 1 hard-boiled egg (chopped, you can also use 1/3 cup of cubed tofu or store-bought egg replacers)
- 1 slice of toast (whole-wheat)
- Salt

Directions:

1. In a bowl, attach the avocado and mash well.

2. Add the lemon juice, celery, and salt, then mix until well incorporated.
3. Fold in the egg until just combined.
4. Spread the mixture on the slice of toast.
5. Enjoy!

Nutrition:

Calories: 160

Fat: 12.7g

Protein: 7.36g

Sodium: 72mg

Total Carbs: 5.25g

26. Healthy Chickpea Scramble Stuffed Sweet Potatoes

Preparation time: 5 minutes

Cooking time: 20 minutes

Servings: 2

Ingredients:

For the scramble:

- 1/2 tsp. avocado oil
- 1/2 tsp. turmeric
- 1 cup of chickpeas (soaked overnight, boiled for an hour, drained, and dried; you can also use canned, but you must first rinse, drain, and dry)
- 1/4 small onion (diced)
- 2 cloves of garlic (minced)
- Sea salt

For the kale:

- 1/2 tsp. avocado oil
- 1/2 tsp. garlic (minced)
- 1 cup of kale leaves (stems removed, cut into small pieces)
- For assembling:
- 1/2 avocado (sliced)
- 2 small sweet potatoes (baked)

Directions:

1. In a pan, add the avocado oil over medium heat, along with the garlic and onions.
2. Cook until softened.
3. Add the chickpeas, turmeric, and salt, then continue cooking for about 10 minutes. To avoid drying the mixture out, you may add teaspoons of water.
4. Mash about 2/3 of the chickpeas using a wooden spoon to make a scrambled texture.
5. Set the pan off the heat and set it aside.
6. In a separate pan, add the avocado oil over medium heat, along with the garlic and kale.
7. Cook until soft, then take the pan off the heat.
8. Slice one baked sweet potato in half and use a spoon to scoop out the center.
9. Spoon half of the chickpea scramble into the baked sweet potato and top with half of the softened kale.
10. Top with half of the avocado slices.
11. Repeat the assembling steps for the other baked sweet potato.
12. Serve and enjoy.

Nutrition:

Calories: 275

Fat: 11.76g

Protein: 8.31g

Sodium: 190mg

Total Carbs: 37.34g

27. High-Protein: Breakfast Bowl

Preparation time: 5 minutes

Cooking time: 0 minutes

Servings: 1

Ingredients

For the breakfast bowl:

- 1 1/2 tbsp. plant-based Protein: powder
- 1/4 cup of blueberries
- 1/4 cup of raspberries
- 1 small banana (sliced)
- 1 small sweet potato (baked)

For the topping:

- Chia seeds
- Hemp hearts

- Other toppings of your choice

Directions:

1. Set out the flesh of the baked sweet potato and place it in a bowl.
2. Use a fork to mash the flesh until you get the consistency you desire.
3. Add the Protein: powder and mix until well combined.
4. Arrange the blueberries, raspberries, and banana slices in layers on top of the mashed sweet potato.
5. Top with your desired toppings.
6. Warm for about 15 minutes before serving.

Nutrition:

Calories: 290

Fat: 0.85g

Protein: 10.36g

Sodium: 190mg

Total Carbs: 65.13g

28. Green Smoothie Bowl

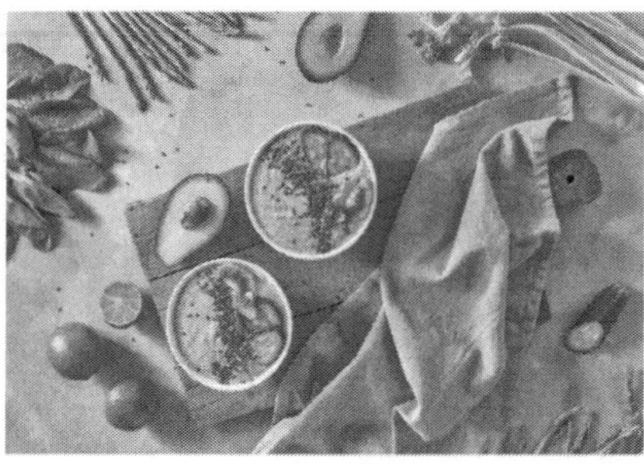

Preparation time: 10 minutes

Cooking time: 0 minutes

Servings: 2

Ingredients:

- 1 cup of fresh strawberries, hulled
- 2 medium ripe bananas, (previously sliced and frozen)
- 1/4 of a ripe avocado (peeled, pitted, and chopped)
- 1 cup of fresh spinach
- 1 cup of fresh kale, trimmed
- 1 tablespoon of flaxseed meal
- 11/2 cups of unsweetened almond milk
- 1/4 cup of almonds
- 1/4 cup of unsweetened coconut, shredded

Direction:

1. Put all ingredients into a high-speed blender except almonds and coconut. Pulse to smoothen.
2. Transfer the puree to bowls and serve immediately with almonds and coconut toppings.

Nutrition:

Calories: 352

Fats: 18.6g

Carbs: 45.3g

Sugar: 19.3g

Proteins: 7.9g

Sodium: 168mg

29. Fruity Bowl

Preparation time: 10 minutes

Cooking time: 0 minutes

Servings: 2

Ingredients:

- 2 cups of frozen cherries (pitted)
- 4 dates (pitted and chopped)
- 1 large apple (peeled, cored, and chopped)
- A cup of fresh cherries pitted
- 2 tablespoons of Chia seeds

Directions:

1. Put frozen cherries and dates in a high-speed blender and pulse.
2. Mix the chopped apple with fresh cherries and Chia seeds in a bowl.
3. Add cherry sauce to the puree and stir.
4. Cover and refrigerate them overnight before serving.

Nutrition:

Calories: 211

Fats: 3.2g

Carbs: 49.7g

Sugar: 35g

Proteins: 3.8g
Sodium: 6mg

30. Quinoa and Pumpkin Porridge

Preparation time: 10 minutes
Cooking time: 12 minutes
Servings: 4
Ingredients:

- 31/2 cups of filtered water
- 13/4 cups of quinoa (soaked for fifteen minutes and rinsed)
- 14 ounces of unsweetened coconut milk
- 13/4 cups of sugar-free pumpkin puree
- 2 teaspoons of ground cinnamon
- 1 teaspoon of ground ginger
- A pinch of ground cloves
- A pinch of ground nutmeg
- Salt
- 3 tablespoons of extra-virgin coconut oil
- 4-6 drops of liquid stevia
- 1 teaspoon of organic vanilla flavor

Directions:

1. Pour water and quinoa into a pan and cook on high heat.
2. Cover the pan and let the produce boil.
3. Set heat to low and simmer for around 12 minutes or until all liquid gets absorbed.
4. Add the remaining ingredients and stir thoroughly.
5. Immediately, remove switch off the cooker, and serve warm.

Nutrition:
Calories: 561
Fats: 29g
Carbs: 60.3g
Sugar: 6.2g
Proteins: 13g
Sodium: 80mg

Chapter 2. Lunch

31. Grilled Avocado Sandwich

Preparation time: 10 minutes
Cooking time: 15 minutes
Servings: 4
Ingredients:

- 8 slices of pumpernickel bread
- 1 cup sauerkraut, drained and rinsed
- 1 cup hummus
- 1 teaspoon dairy-free margarine
- 1 avocado sliced into 16 pieces

Directions:

1. Preheat your oven to 450 degrees F.
2. Apply margarine on one side of your bread slices.
3. Keep 4 slices on your baking sheet. The margarine side should be down.
4. Distribute half of the hummus over the bread slices.
5. Place sauerkraut on the hummus.
6. Keep avocado slices over your sauerkraut.
7. Spread hummus on the remaining slices.
8. Keep the hummus side down on your slices of avocado.
9. Bake for 7 minutes.
10. Set over and bake for another 6 minutes.

Nutrition
Calories 340
Carbohydrates 39g
Total Fat 16g
Protein 10g
Fiber 11g
Sugar 1g
Sodium 781mg
Potassium 552mg

32. Cauliflower Steaks with Tamarind and Beans

Preparation time: 20 minutes
Cooking time: 50 minutes
Servings: 2
Ingredients:

- 1/2 cup of olive oil
- 1/5 lb. cauliflower head
- 1 teaspoon black pepper, ground
- 2 teaspoons of kosher salt
- 3 cloves of garlic, chopped
- 1/2 lb. green beans, trimmed
- 1/3 cup parsley, chopped
- 3/4 teaspoon lemon zest, grated
- 1/5 lb. parmesan, grated
- 1/4 lb. panko breadcrumbs
- 1/3 cup tamarind
- 1 lb. white beans, rinsed and drained
- 1 teaspoon of Dijon mustard
- 2 tablespoons of margarine

Directions:

1. Warmth your oven to 425 F. Take out the leaves and trim the stem ends of your cauliflower. Keep the core side down on your working surface.
2. Slice from the center top to down with a knife. Keep it on a baking sheet. Apply 1 tablespoon oil on both sides. Season with pepper and salt. Roast for 30 minutes. Turn halfway through.
3. Toss the green beans in the meantime with 1 tablespoon of oil and pepper. Keep on your baking sheet in a single layer. Roast for 15 minutes.
4. Whisk the lemon zest, garlic, parsley, salt, pepper, and oil together in a bowl. Keep half of this mix in another bowl. Add Parmesan and panko to

the first bowl. Use your hands to mix. Add tamarind and white beans to the second bowl. Coat well by tossing. Now whisk together the mustard and margarine.

5. Spread your margarine mix over the cauliflower. Sprinkle the panko mix over the cauliflower. Add the white bean mix to the sheet with beans. Combine. Keep sheet in the oven and roast for 5 minutes.

6. Divide the beans, cauliflower, and tamarind among plates.

Nutrition

Calories 1366

Carbohydrates 166g

Cholesterol 6mg

Total Fat 67g

Protein 59g

Fiber 41g

Sugar 20g

Sodium 2561mg

33. Smoked Salmon Tartine

Preparation time: 20 minutes

Cooking time: 20 minutes

Servings: 2

Ingredients:

- 1/3 pumpkin
- 2 tablespoons of dairy-free margarine
- 1-1/2 tablespoons chives, minced
- 1/4 lb. cashew paste
- Thinly sliced smoked salmon
- 1/2 clove of garlic, minced
- 1/2 lemon zest
- 2 tablespoons red onion, chopped
- 2 tablespoons capers, drained
- 1/2 boiled egg, chopped
- Black pepper and kosher salt

Directions:

1. Bring together the lemon zest, garlic and cashew paste in a bowl. Season with pepper and salt. Stir in the chives gently and set aside. Now season the boiled egg and red onion with salt. Grate your pumpkin.

2. Squeeze the pumpkin and remove any excess liquid. Season with pepper and salt. Heat the margarine over medium temperature. Add the pumpkin. Use a spatula to shape roughly into a circle.

3. Use the backside of a spoon to press on your mixture. Cook covered for 10 minutes. Flip and cook for another 8 minutes. It should be crispy and golden brown. Take out and let it cool.

4. Spread the paste mix on top. Layer your smoked salmon over this. Sprinkle with capers, the boiled egg, and red onion. Garnish with chives. Cut into small wedges before serving.

Nutrition

Calories 734

Carbohydrates 37g

Cholesterol 115mg

Total Fat 54g

Protein 25g

Sugar 3g

Fiber 5g

Sodium 1641mg

34. Healthy Chicken Marsala

Preparation time: 15 minutes

Cooking time: 30 minutes

Servings: 4

Ingredients:

- 1-1/2 chicken breasts, boneless and skinless
- 2 tablespoons of dairy-free margarine
- 1/2 lb. shiitake mushrooms, sliced and stemmed
- 1 lb. baby Bella mushrooms, sliced and stemmed
- 2 tablespoons of extra virgin olive oil
- 3 cloves of garlic, chopped
- 1 cup shallot, chopped
- 2 cups of chicken broth, low-sodium
- 3/4 cup dry marsala wine

- Black pepper, kosher salt, chopped parsley leaves

Directions:

1. Dry your chicken breasts using a paper towel. Slice them horizontally into half. Keep each piece between parchment paper. Use your meat mallet to pound until you have 1/4 inch thickness. Season all sides with black pepper and kosher salt.
2. Dredge in some whole wheat flour. Keep aside. Heat your skillet over medium temperature. Pour olive oil and margarine in your pan. Sauté the chicken for 5 minutes. Work in batches, not overcrowding your pan. Transfer to a baking sheet. Set aside.
3. Wipe off excess cooking fat from your pan. Bring back to heat. Add the remaining margarine and the mushrooms. Sauté over high temperature. Season with black pepper and salt. Add the garlic and chopped shallot to your pan.
4. Sauté 3 minutes. Include the marsala wine. Bring down the heat for a minute. Include the chicken broth and cook for 5 minutes. Transfer chicken cutlets to the pan. Spoon over the sauce.
5. Garnish with parsley.

Nutrition

Calories 546

Carbohydrates 41g

Cholesterol 31mg

Total Fat 38g

Protein 10g

Sugar 6g

Fiber 5g

Sodium 535mg

35. Grilled Salmon Burgers

Preparation time: 10 minutes

Cooking time: 10 minutes

Servings: 4

Ingredients:

- 1 lb. salmon fillet, skinless and cubed
- 1 tablespoon Dijon mustard
- 1 tablespoon lime peel, grated
- 1 tablespoon ginger, peeled and minced
- 1 tablespoon cilantro, chopped
- 1 teaspoon soy sauce, low-sodium
- 1/2 teaspoon coriander, ground
- Cilantro leaves and lime wedges
- Pepper and salt to taste

Directions:

1. Preheat your barbecue grill on medium heat. Apply cooking spray on the grill's rack lightly. Pulse the salmon in your food processor. It should grind coarsely.
2. Take out the salmon and keep in a bowl. Mix in the lime peel, mustard, cilantro, ginger, coriander, and soy sauce. Create 4 patties. Season with pepper and salt.
3. Grill your burgers, turning once on medium heat. 4 minutes for each side. Garnish with cilantro leaves and lime wedges.

Nutrition

Calories: 395

Cholesterol: 60 mg

Carbohydrates: 1 g

Fat: 7 g

Sugar: 0 g
Fiber: 0 g
Protein: 23 g

36. Tuna Steaks

Preparation time: 15 minutes
Cooking time: 15 minutes
Servings: 2
Ingredients:

- 1-1/2 cups water
- 1 tablespoon lemon juice
- Pepper and salt to taste
- 1 teaspoon cayenne pepper
- 2 tuna steaks
- 3 kumquats, seeded, sliced, rinsed
- 1/3 cup cilantro, chopped

Directions:

1. Mix lemon juice, cayenne pepper and water over medium heat in a saucepan.
2. Season with pepper and salt. Boil.
3. Now include the tuna steaks into this mix.
4. Sprinkle cilantro and kumquats.
5. Cook for 15 minutes. The fish should flake easily with your fork.

Nutrition
Calories: 141
Cholesterol: 50 mg
Carbohydrates: 6 g
Fat: 1 g
Sugar: 3 g
Fiber: 2 g
Protein: 27 g

37. Air Fryer Salmon

Preparation time: 6 minutes
Cooking time: 5 minutes
Servings: 2
Ingredients:

- 1/3 lb. filets of salmon
- 1/4 cup of margarine
- 1/4 cup of pistachios, chopped finely
- 1-1/2 tablespoons of minced dill
- 2 tablespoons of lemon juice

Directions:

1. Warmth your air fryer to 400 degrees F. Spray olive oil on the basket. Season your salmon with pepper to taste. You can also apply the all-purpose seasoning. Combine the margarine, lemon juice, and dill in a bowl.
2. Pour a spoonful on the fillets. Top the fillets with chopped pistachios. Be generous. Spray olive oil on the salmon lightly. Air fry your fillets now for 5 minutes.
3. Take out the salmon carefully with a spatula from your air fryer. Keep on a plate. Garnish with dill.

Nutrition
Calories 305
Carbohydrates 1g
Cholesterol 43mg
Total Fat 21g
Protein 28g
Fiber 2g
Sugar 3g
Sodium 92mg

38. Rosemary Garlic Lamb Chops

Preparation time: 3 minutes
Cooking time: 10 minutes
Servings 2
Ingredients:

- 4 chops of lamb
- 1 teaspoon olive oil
- 2 teaspoon garlic puree
- Fresh garlic
- Fresh rosemary

Directions:

1. Keep your lamb chops in the fryer grill pan. Season the chops with pepper and salt. Brush some olive oil. Add some garlic puree on each chop.
2. Cover the grill pan gaps with garlic cloves and rosemary sprigs. Refrigerate to marinate. Take out after 1 hour. Keep in the fryer and cook for 5 minutes.

3. Use your spatula to turn the chops over. Add some olive oil and cook for another 5 minutes. Set aside for a minute. Take out the rosemary and garlic before serving.

Nutrition

Calories 678

Carbohydrates 1g

Cholesterol 257mg

Total Fat 38g

Protein 83g

Sugar 0g

Sodium 200mg

39. Mushroom Farro Risotto

Preparation time: 15 minutes

Cooking time: 60 minutes

Servings: 5

Ingredients:

- 3 tablespoons of melted coconut oil
- 4 cups chicken broth, low sodium
- 3/4 lb. baby Bella mushrooms, trimmed and sliced
- 1/2 yellow onion, chopped
- 3 cloves of garlic, chopped
- 1 tablespoon thyme, chopped
- 3/4 cup of dry white wine
- 1-1/2 cups organic farro
- 1 teaspoon lemon juice
- 3/4 cup vegan parmesan
- 3/4 cup peas
- Ground black pepper, kosher salt, chopped parsley

Directions:

1. Keep your chicken broth in a saucepan. Simmer over low heat. Heat the coconut oil over medium temperature in a pot. Add kosher salt and onion. Sauté for 6 minutes. Stir often.
2. Bring up the heat to high. Now add the mushrooms. Combine by stirring. Cook for another 2 minutes. The mushrooms should become soft. Add the thyme and garlic. Sauté for a minute, stirring occasionally. Include the toast and farro and cook for 1 more minute. Keep stirring.
3. Pour in the white wine. Cook for 3 minutes. Stir often. The wine needs to be absorbed completely. Add the hot broth to your pot. Combine well. Bring down the heat and cook for 45 minutes. Stir every 15 minutes.
4. Add the lemon juice and grated parmesan. Stir to combine. Fold in the peas. Season with pepper and salt. Take out the pot from heat. Let it sit covered for 5 minutes.
5. Garnish with thyme leaves and parsley.

Nutrition

Calories 397

Carbohydrates 29g

Cholesterol 32mg

Total Fat 25g

Protein 14g

Sugar 5g

Fiber 5g

Sodium 429mg

40. Instant Pot Black Beans

Preparation time: 15 minutes

Cooking time: 15 minutes

Servings: 8

Ingredients:

- 2 cups of black beans, rinsed and dried
- 1 yellow onion, chopped
- 2 tablespoons of extra virgin olive oil
- 2 garlic cloves, smashed
- 1 jalapeno pepper, sliced

- 1 red bell pepper, stemmed and seeded
- 1 handful of cilantro
- 1/2 teaspoon of red pepper flakes
- 2 teaspoons cumin, ground
- 2 teaspoons kosher salt

Directions:

1. Keep the black beans in your saucepan. Cover with cold water for 6 hours. Drain and rinse.
2. Heat oil and add the garlic, onions, and salt. Sauté for 5 minutes.
3. Add the jalapeno, bell pepper, red pepper flakes, black pepper, and cumin. Sauté for another 3 minutes. Stir frequently. Now include the cilantro stems, beans, water, and some more salt. Combine well by stirring. Cook for 7 minutes. Release naturally.

Nutrition
Calories 144
Carbohydrates 14g
Cholesterol 0mg
Total Fat 8g
Protein 4g
Sugar 1g
Fiber 4g
Sodium 606mg

41. Popcorn Chicken

Preparation time: 15 minutes
Cooking time: 10 minutes
Servings: 4
Ingredients:

- 1/5 lb. chicken breast halves, boneless and skinless
- 1/2 teaspoon paprika
- 1/4 teaspoon mustard, ground
- 1/4 teaspoon of garlic powder
- 3 tablespoons of arrowroot

Directions:

1. Divide the chicken into small pieces and keep in a bowl. Combine the paprika, garlic powder, mustard, salt, and pepper in another bowl. Reserve a teaspoon of your seasoning mixture. Sprinkle the other portion on the chicken. Coat evenly by tossing.
2. Combine the reserved seasoning and arrowroot in a plastic bag. Combine well by shaking. Keep your chicken pieces in the bag. Seal it and shake for coating evenly. Now transfer the chicken to a mesh strainer. Shake the excess arrowroot.
3. Keep aside for 5-10 minutes. The arrowroot should start to get absorbed into your chicken. Warmth your air fryer to 390 degrees F. Apply some oil on the air fryer basket.
4. Keep the chicken pieces inside. They should not overlap. Apply cooking spray. Cook until the chicken isn't pink anymore.

Nutrition
Calories 156
Carbohydrates 6g
Cholesterol 65mg
Total Fat 4g
Protein 24g
Sugar 0g
Fiber 1g
Sodium 493mg

42. Banana Bread

Preparation time: 15 minutes
Cooking time: 45 minutes
Servings: 8
Ingredients:

- 3/4 cup whole wheat flour
- 2 medium ripe mashed bananas
- 2 large eggs
- 1 teaspoon of Vanilla extract
- 1/4 teaspoon baking soda
- 1/2 cup stevia

Directions:

1. Set your parchment paper at the bottom of your pan. Apply some cooking spray. Whisk together the baking soda, salt, flour, and cinnamon (optional) in a bowl.
2. Keep it aside. Take another bowl and bring together the eggs, bananas, and vanilla in it.

3. Stir the wet ingredients gently into your flour mix. Combine well. Now pour your batter into the pan. You can also sprinkle some walnuts.
4. Heat your air fryer to 310F. Cook till it turns brown. Keep the bread on your wire rack so that it cools in the pan. Slice.

Nutrition
Calories 240
Carbohydrates 29g
Total Fat 12g
Protein 4g
Fiber 2g
Sodium 184mg
Sugar 17g

43. Pumpkin Protein Bowl

Preparation time: 5 minutes
Cooking time: 5 minutes
Servings: 1
Ingredients:

- 1/2 lb. pumpkin, already baked
- 1 banana, sliced
- 1/10 lb. protein powder scoop
- 1/4 cup blueberries
- 1/4 cup raspberries

Directions:

1. Grate the pumpkin.
2. Stir in the protein powder. Combine well.
3. Now layer the banana slices, blueberries, and raspberries.
4. You can add toppings like nuts, hemp hearts, and chia seeds.

Nutrition
Calories 348
Carbohydrates 67g
Cholesterol 0mg
Total Fat 2g
Protein 28g
Fiber 19g
Sodium 8mg
Sugar 24g

44. Baked French Toast Casserole

Preparation time: 20 minutes
Cooking time: 45 minutes
Servings: 12
Ingredients:

- 1 lb. French bread
- 1 cup of egg white liquid
- 6 eggs
- 1/3 cup maple syrup
- 1-1/2 cups of rice milk,
- 1/2 lb. raspberries
- 1/2 lb. blueberries
- 1 teaspoon of vanilla extract
- 3/4 cup strawberries

Directions:

1. Slice the bread into small cubes. Keep them in a greased casserole dish. Add all the berries. Only leave a few for the topping. Set together the egg whites, eggs, rice milk, and maple syrup in a bowl. Combine well.
2. Set the egg mix over the top of the bread. Press the bread down. All pieces should be soaked well. Add berries on the top. Fill up the holes, if any. Refrigerate secured for a couple of hours at least.
3. Set out the casserole half an hour before baking. Set your oven to 350 degrees F.
4. Bake your casserole uncovered for 30 minutes. Bake for another 15 minutes secured with a foil.
5. Let it rest for 15 minutes. Serve it warm with maple syrup.

Nutrition

Calories 200
Carbohydrates 31g
Cholesterol 93mg
Total Fat 4g
Protein 10g
Fiber 2g
Sodium 288mg
Sugar 10g

45. Whole Grain Blueberry Scones

Preparation time: 10 minutes
Cooking time: 25 minutes
Servings: 8
Ingredients:

- 2 cups of whole-wheat flour
- 1/4 cup maple syrup
- 6 tablespoons of olive oil
- 2-1/2 teaspoons baking powder
- 1/2 teaspoon see salt
- 2 tablespoons of coconut milk
- 1 teaspoon vanilla extract
- 1 cup blueberries

Directions:

1. Warmth your oven to 400 degrees F. Keep parchment paper on your baking sheet. Attach the syrup, flour, salt, and baking powder in a bowl. Blend well by whisking together.
2. Set the olive oil into a bowl with the dry ingredients.
3. Work the oil into your flour mix.
4. Whisk the vanilla extract and coconut milk into the dry ingredients bowl.
5. Fold in the blueberries gently. Your dough should be sticky and thick. Apply some flour to your hands and shape the dough into a circle.
6. Take a knife and create triangle slices. Keep them on the baking sheet. Maintain an 8-inch gap.
7. Bake for 25 minutes. Set aside for cooling once done.

Nutrition
Calories 331
Carbohydrates 27g
Cholesterol 0mg
Total Fat 23g
Protein 4g
Fiber 4g
Sugar 8g

46. Pan-Seared Scallops with Lemon-Ginger Vinaigrette

Preparation Time: 10 minutes
Cooking Time: 7 minutes
Servings: 4
Ingredients:

- 2 tbsps. extra virgin olive oil
- 1 1/2 pound sea scallop
- 1/2 tsp. sea salt
- 1/8 tsp. freshly ground black pepper
- 1/4 cup lemon ginger vinaigrette

Directions:

1. In a big nonstick skillet at medium-high heat, heat the olive oil until it shimmers.
2. Flavor the scallops with pepper and salt and add them to the skillet. Cook per side until just opaque.
3. Serve with the vinaigrette set over the top.

Nutrition:
Calories: 280
Total Fat: 16
Total carbs: 5 g
Sugar: 1 g
Fiber: 0 g

Protein: 29 g
Sodium: 508 mg

47. Manhattan-Style Salmon Chowder

Preparation Time: 10 minutes
Cooking Time: 15 minutes
Servings: 4
Ingredients:

- 1/4 cup extra virgin olive oil
- 1 red bell pepper, chopped
- 1 pound skinless salmon. pin bones removed, chopped into 1/2 inch
- 2 cans crushed tomatoes, 1 drained, 1 undrained
- 6 cups no-salt-added chicken broth
- 2 cups diced sweet potato
- 1 tsp. onion powder
- 1/2 tsp. sea salt
- 1/4 tsp. freshly ground black pepper

Directions:

1. Attach the red bell pepper and salmon. Cook for at least 5 minutes, until the fish is opaque and the bell pepper is soft.
2. Whisk in the tomatoes, chicken broth, sweet potatoes, onion powder, salt, and pepper. Set to a simmer, then lower the heat to medium. Cook for at least 10 minutes, until the sweet potatoes are soft.

Nutrition:
Calories: 570
Total Fat: 42
Total carbs: 55 g
Sugar: 24 g
Fiber: 16 g
Protein: 41 g
Sodium: 1.29 mg

48. Sesame-Tuna Skewers

Preparation Time: 10 minutes
Cooking Time: 15 minutes
Servings: 6
Ingredients:

- 6 oz. cubed thick tuna steaks
- Cooking spray
- 1/4 tsp. ground black pepper.
- 3/4 cup sesame seeds
- 1 tsp. salt
- 1/2 tsp. ground ginger.
- 2 tbsps. toasted sesame oil

Directions:

1. Preheat the oven to about 400F. Set a rimmed baking tray with cooking spray.
2. Plume twelve wooden skewers in water. In a mixing bowl, merge pepper, ground ginger, salt, and sesame seeds. In another bowl, set the tuna with sesame oil.
3. Set the oiled cubes into a sesame seed mixture and set the cubes on each skewer.
4. Place the skewers on a readily prepared baking tray and put the tray into the preheated oven.
5. Bake for 12 minutes and turn once.
6. Serve.

Nutrition:
Calories: 196
Protein: 14.47 g
Fat: 15.01 g
Carbs: 2.48 g

49. Trout with Chard

Preparation Time: 10 minutes
Cooking Time: 15 minutes
Servings: 4
Ingredients:

- 1/2 cup vegetable broth
- 2 bunches of sliced chard
- 4 boneless trout fillets
- Salt
- 1 tbsp. extra virgin olive oil
- 2 minced garlic cloves
- 1/4 cup golden raisins
- Ground black pepper
- 1 chopped onion
- 1 tbsp. apple cider vinegar

Directions:

1. Preheat the oven to about 375F. Attach seasonings to the trout
2. Set olive oil in a pan, then heat. Attach garlic and onion, then sauté for 3 minutes.
3. Attach chard to sauté for 2 more minutes. Attach broth, raisins, and cedar vinegar to the pan.
4. Set a topping of trout fillets Secure the pan and put it in the preheated oven for 10 minutes.
5. Serve and enjoy.

Nutrition:
Calories: 284
Protein: 2.07 g
Fat: 30.32 g
Carbs: 3.49 g

50. Seafood Noodles

Preparation Time: 10 minutes
Cooking Time: 20 minutes
Servings: 2
Ingredients:

- Braised olive oil
- 4 garlic cloves, minced
- 300 g clean squid cut into rings
- 200 g mussel without shell
- 200 g shell-less volley
- 10 clean prawns
- 150 g dried tomatoes
- Salt to taste
- black pepper to taste
- 500 g pre-cooked noodles
- 1/2 pack watercress
- 1/2 Lemon Juice
- parsley to taste

Directions:

1. In olive oil, set the garlic and add the squid, the mussel, the shrimp, and the shrimp.
2. Set the dried tomatoes and season with salt and pepper.
3. Attach the noodles, watercress, season with lemon juice and parsley.

Nutrition:
Calories: 2049
Protein: 56.21 g
Fat: 143.36 g
Carbs: 139.98 g

51. Spicy Pulled Chicken Wraps

Preparation Time: 15 minutes
Cooking Time: 6 to 8 hours
Servings: 4
Ingredients:

- 1 romaine lettuce head
- 1 1/2 tsp. ground cumin
- 1 1/2 cup low-fat, low-sodium chicken broth
- 1 tsp. paprika
- 1 tsp. garlic powder
- 1 lb. skinless, deboned chicken breasts
- 2 tsps. chili powder

Directions:

1. In a slow cooker, put all the ingredients except lettuce and gently stir to combine.
2. Set the slow cooker on low.
3. Cover and cook for about 6-8 hours.
4. Unsecure the slow cooker and transfer the breasts to a large plate.
5. With a fork, shred the breasts.
6. Serve the shredded beef over lettuce leaves.

Nutrition:
Calories: 150
Fat: 3.4 g
Carbs: 12 g
Protein: 14 g
Sugars: 7 g
Sodium: 900 mg

52. Apricot Chicken Wings

Preparation Time: 15 minutes
Cooking Time: 45-60 minutes
Servings: 3-4
Ingredients:

- 1 medium jar apricot preserve
- 1 package Lipton onion dry soup mix
- 1 medium bottle Russian dressing
- 2 lbs. chicken wings

Directions:

1. Preheat the oven to 350F.
2. Clean and pat dry the chicken wings.
3. Set the chicken wings on a baking pan, single layer.
4. Bake until turning halfway.
5. In a bowl, merge the Lipton® soup mix, apricot preserve, and Russian dressing.
6. Once the wings are cooked, et with the sauce, until the pieces are coated.
7. Serve immediately with a side dish.

Nutrition:
Calories: 162
Fat: 17 g
Carbs: 76 g
Protein: 13 g
Sugars: 24 g
Sodium: 700 mg

53. Champion Chicken Pockets

Preparation Time: 5 minutes
Cooking Time: 0 minutes
Servings: 4
Ingredients:

- 1/2 cup chopped broccoli
- 2 halved whole wheat pita bread rounds
- 1/4 cup bottled reduced-fat ranch salad dressing
- 1/4 cup chopped pecans or walnuts
- 1 1/2 cup chopped cooked chicken
- 1/4 cup plain low-fat yogurt
- 1/4 cup shredded carrot

Directions:

1. In a bowl, set together yogurt and ranch salad dressing, then mix.
2. In a medium bowl, combine chicken, broccoli, carrot, and, if desired, nuts. Pour yogurt mixture over chicken; toss to coat.
3. Spoon chicken mixture into pita halves.

Nutrition:
Calories: 384

Fat: 11.4 g
Carbs: 7.4 g
Protein: 59.3 g
Sugars: 1.3 g
Sodium: 368.7 mg

54. Chicken-Bell Pepper Sauté

Preparation Time: 10 minutes
Cooking Time: 30 minutes
Servings: 6
Ingredients:

- 1 tbsp. olive oil
- 1 sliced large yellow bell pepper
- 1 sliced large red bell pepper
- 3 cup onion sliced crosswise
- 6 4-oz skinless, boneless chicken breast halves
- Cooking spray
- 20 Kalamata olives
- 1/4 tsp. Freshly ground black pepper
- 1/2 tsp. salt
- 2 tbsps. finely chopped fresh flat-leaf parsley
- 2 1/3 cup coarsely chopped tomato
- 1 tsp. chopped fresh oregano

Directions:

1. Set your heat to medium-high and set non-stick frying in place. Warmth the oil. Sauté the onions for 8 minutes once the oil is hot.
2. Attach bell pepper and sauté for 10 more minutes.
3. Attach tomato, salt, and black pepper to cook for about 7 minutes until the tomato juice has evaporated.
4. Attach parsley, oregano, and olives to cook for 2 minutes until heated. Set into a bowl and keep warm.
5. Using a paper towel, wipe the pan and grease with cooking spray. Cook on each of the sides.
6. When cooking the last batch, attach back the previous batch of chicken and onion-bell pepper mixture, then cook.
7. Serve warm and enjoy.

Nutrition:
Calories: 223
Protein: 28.13 g
Fat: 7.82 g
Carbs: 9.5 g

55. Curried Beef Meatballs

Preparation Time: 20 minutes
Cooking Time: 22 minutes
Servings: 6
Ingredients:
For Meatballs:

- 1 pound lean ground beef
- 2 organic eggs, beaten
- 3 tbsps. red onion, minced
- 1/4 cup fresh basil leaves, chopped
- 1 (1-inch) fresh ginger piece, chopped finely
- 4 garlic cloves, chopped finely
- 3 Thai birds-eye chilies, minced
- 1 tsp. coconut sugar
- 1 tbsp. red curry paste
- Salt, to taste
- 1 tbsp. fish sauce
- 2 tbsps. coconut oil

For Curry:

- 1 red onion, chopped
- Salt, to taste
- 4 garlic cloves, minced

- 1 (1-inch) fresh ginger piece, minced
- 2 Thai birds-eye chilies, minced
- 2 tbsps. red curry paste
- 1 (14 oz.) coconut milk
- Salt, to taste
- Freshly ground black pepper, to taste
- Lime wedges (as desired)

Directions:

1. For meatballs in a big bowl, put all the ingredients except oil and mix until well combined.
2. Make small balls from the mixture.
3. In a big skillet, melt coconut oil on medium heat.
4. Attach meatballs and cook for about 3-5 minutes or till golden brown on all sides.
5. Transfer the meatballs right into a bowl.
6. In the same skillet, attach onion and a pinch of salt and sauté for around 5 minutes.
7. Attach garlic, ginger, and chilies, and sauté for about 1 minute.
8. Attach curry paste and sauté for around 1 minute.
9. Attach coconut milk and meatballs and convey to some gentle simmer.
10. Set the warmth to low and simmer, covered for around 10 minutes.
11. Serve using the topping of lime wedges.

Nutrition:

Calories: 444

Fat: 15 g

Carbs: 20 g

Fiber: 2 g

Protein: 37 g

56. Beef Meatballs in Tomato Gravy

Preparation Time: 20 minutes

Cooking Time: 37 minutes

Servings: 4

Ingredients:

For Meatballs:

- 1 pound lean ground beef
- 1 organic egg, beaten
- 1 tbsp. fresh ginger, minced
- 1 garlic oil, minced
- 2 tbsps. fresh cilantro, chopped finely
- 2 tbsps. tomato paste
- 1/3 cup almond meal
- 1 tbsp. ground cumin
- A pinch of ground cinnamon
- Salt, to taste
- Freshly ground black pepper, to taste
- 1/4 cup coconut oil

For Tomato Gravy:

- 2 tbsps. coconut oil
- 1/2 small onion, chopped
- 2 garlic cloves, chopped
- 1 tsp. fresh lemon zest, grated finely
- 2 cups tomatoes, chopped finely
- A pinch of ground cinnamon
- 1 tsp. red pepper flakes, crushed
- 3/4 cup chicken broth
- Salt, to taste
- Freshly ground black pepper, to taste
- 1/4 cup fresh parsley, chopped

Directions:

1. For meatballs in a bowl, attach all ingredients except oil and mix until well combined.
2. Set about 1-inch sized balls from the mixture.
3. In a substantial skillet, melt coconut oil into medium heat.
4. Attach meatballs and cook for approximately 3-5 minutes or till golden brown on all sides.
5. Set the meatballs into a bowl.
6. For gravy in a pan, melt coconut oil into medium heat.
7. Attach onion and garlic and sauté for approximately 4 minutes.
8. Attach lemon zest and sauté for approximately 1 minute.

9. Attach tomatoes, cinnamon, red pepper flakes, and broth and simmer for approximately 7 minutes.
10. Whisk in salt, black pepper, and meatballs and reduce the warmth to medium-low.
11. Simmer for approximately twenty minutes.
12. Serve hot.

Nutrition:
Calories: 404
Fat: 11 g
Carbs: 27 g
Fiber: 4 g
Protein: 38 g

57. Pork with Lemongrass

Preparation Time: 10 minutes
Cooking Time: 30 minutes
Servings: 4
Ingredients:

- 4 pork chops
- 2 tbsps. olive oil
- 2 spring onions, chopped
- A pinch of salt and black pepper
- 1/2 cup vegetable stock
- 1 stalk lemongrass, chopped
- 2 tbsps. coconut aminos
- 2 tbsps. cilantro, chopped

Directions:
1. Warmth a pan with the oil on medium-high heat, add the spring onions, and the meat, and brown for 5 minutes.
2. Attach the rest of the ingredients, toss, and cook everything over medium heat for 25 minutes.
3. Divide the mix between plates and serve.

Nutrition:
Calories: 290
Fat: 4 g
Fiber: 6 g
Carbs: 8 g
Protein: 14 g

58. Pork with Olives

Preparation Time: 10 minutes
Cooking Time: 40 minutes
Servings: 4
Ingredients:

- 1 yellow onion, chopped
- 4 pork chops
- 2 tbsps. olive oil
- 1 tbsp. sweet paprika
- 2 tbsps. balsamic vinegar
- 1/4 cup Kalamata olives
- 1 tbsp. cilantro, chopped
- A pinch of Sea Salt
- A pinch of black pepper

Directions:
1. Warmth a pan with the oil on medium heat; add the onion and sauté for 5 minutes.
2. Attach the meat and brown for a further 5 minutes.
3. Set the rest of the ingredients, toss, cook over medium heat for 30 minutes, divide between plates and serve.

Nutrition:
Calories: 280
Fat: 11 g
Fiber: 6 g
Carbs: 10 g
Protein: 21 g

59. Avocado-Orange Grilled Chicken

Preparation Time: 10 minutes
Cooking Time: 12 minutes
Servings: 4
Ingredients:

- 1 cup low-fat yogurt
- Salt
- 4 pieces of 4-6oz boneless, skinless chicken breasts
- 2 tbsps. chopped cilantro
- 1 tbsp. honey
- 1 thinly sliced small red onion
- 1/4 cup fresh lime juice
- 1 deseeded avocado, peeled and chopped
- 2 peeled and sectioned oranges
- Pepper
- 1/4 cup minced red onion

Directions:

1. Set up a mixing bowl and merge yogurt, minced red onion, cilantro, and honey. Attach chicken into the mixture and marinate for half an hour. Set grate and preheat the grill to medium-high heat.
2. Set the chicken aside and add seasonings. Grill for 6 minutes on each side.
3. Set the avocado in a bowl. Attach lime juice and toss avocado to coat well.
4. Attach oranges, thinly sliced onions, and cilantro into the bowl with avocado and merge well.
5. Serve avocado dressing alongside grilled chicken.
6. Enjoy.

Nutrition:
Calories: 216
Protein: 8.83 g
Fat: 11.48 g
Carbs: 21.86 g

60. Honey Chicken Tagine

Preparation Time: 60 minutes
Cooking Time: 25 minutes
Servings: 12
Ingredients:

- 1 tbsp. extra virgin olive oil
- 1 tsp. ground coriander
- 1 tbsp. Minced fresh ginger
- 1/2 tsp. ground pepper
- 2 thinly sliced onions
- 12 oz. seeded and roughly chopped kumquats
- 14 oz. vegetable broth
- 1/8 tsp. Ground cloves
- 1/2 tsp. salt
- 1 1/2 tbsps. honey
- 1 tsp. ground cumin
- 2 lbs. boneless, skinless chicken thighs
- 4 slivered garlic cloves
- 15 oz. rinsed chickpeas
- 3/4 tsp. ground cinnamon

Directions:

1. Preheat the oven to about 375F. Set a heatproof casserole on medium heat and heat the oil.
2. Attach onions to sauté for 4 minutes.
3. Attach garlic and ginger to sauté for 1 minute.
4. Attach coriander, cumin, cloves, salt, pepper, and cloves seasonings. Sauté for a minute.
5. Attach kumquats, broth, chickpeas, and honey, then bring to a boil before turning off the heat.
6. Set the casserole in the oven. Bake as you stir at a 15-minute interval. Serve and enjoy.

Nutrition:
Calories: 586
Protein: 15.5 g
Fat: 40.82 g
Carbs: 43.56 g

Chapter 3. Dinner

61. Chicken Bone Broth

Preparation Time: 10 minutes
Cooking Time: 90 minutes
Servings: 8
Ingredients:

- Bones from a 3–4 pound chicken
- 4 cups water
- 2 large carrots, cut into chunks
- 2 large stalks celery
- 1 large onion
- fresh rosemary sprigs
- 3 fresh thyme springs
- 2 tablespoons apple cider vinegar
- 1 teaspoon kosher salt

Directions:

1. Put all the ingredients and allow it to sit for 30 minutes.
2. Pressure cook and adjust the time to 90 minutes.
3. Pressure release naturally until float valve drops and then unlock lid.
4. Strain the broth and transfer into a storage container. The broth can be refrigerated three to five days or frozen up to six months.

Nutrition:
Calories: 44 kcal
Fat: 1 g
Protein: 7 g
Sodium: 312 mg
Fiber: 0 g
Carbohydrates: 0 g
Sugar: 0 g

62. Chicken Bone Broth with Ginger and Lemon

Preparation Time: 10 minutes
Cooking Time: 90 minutes
Servings: 8
Ingredients:

- Bones from a 3–4 pound chicken
- 8 cups water
- 2 large carrots, cut into chunks
- 2 large stalks celery
- 1 large onion
- 3 fresh rosemary sprigs
- 3 fresh thyme springs
- 2 tablespoons apple cider vinegar
- 1 teaspoon kosher salt
- 1-1/2 inches piece fresh ginger, sliced (peeling not necessary)
- 1 large lemon, cut into fourths

Directions:

1. Put all the ingredients in it and allow it to sit for 30 minutes.
2. Pressure cook and adjust the time to 90 minutes.
3. Set the broth using a fine-mesh strainer and transfer it into a storage container.
4. Can be refrigerated for five days or frozen for six months.

Nutrition:
Calories: 44 kcal
Fat: 1 g
Protein: 7 g
Sodium: 312 mg
Fiber: 0 g
Carbohydrates: 0 g
Sugar: 0 g

63. Vegetable Stock

Preparation Time: 10 minutes
Cooking Time: 40 minutes
Servings: 8
Ingredients:

- 2 large carrots
- 1 large onion
- 2 large stalks celery
- 8 ounces white mushrooms
- 5 whole cloves garlic
- 2 cups parsley leaves
- 2 bay leaves
- 2 teaspoons whole black peppercorns
- 2 teaspoons kosher salt
- 10 cups water

Directions:

1. Place all the ingredients in it. Secure the lid.
2. Pressure cook and adjust the time to 40 minutes.
3. Set the broth using a fine-mesh strainer and transfer it into a storage container.

Nutrition:
Calories: 9 kcal
Fat: 0 g
Protein: 0 g
Sodium: 585 mg
Fiber: 0 g
Carbohydrates: 2 g
Sugar: 1 g

64. Chicken Vegetable Soup

Preparation Time: 23 minutes
Cooking Time: 15 minutes
Servings: 8
Ingredients:

- 2 tablespoons avocado oil
- 1 small yellow onion, peeled and chopped
- 2 large carrots, peeled and chopped
- 2 large stalks celery, ends removed and sliced
- 3 cloves garlic, minced
- 1 teaspoon dried thyme
- 1 teaspoon salt
- 8 cups chicken stock
- 3 boneless, skinless, frozen chicken breasts

Directions:

1. Heat the oil for 1 minute. Add the onion, carrots, and celery and sauté for 8 minutes.
2. Add the garlic, thyme, and salt and sauté for another 30 seconds. Press the Cancel button.
3. Add the stock and frozen chicken breasts to the pot. Secure the lid.
4. Pressure Cook and adjust the time to 6 minutes.
5. Allow cooling into bowls to serve.

Nutrition:
Calories: 209 kcal
Fat: 7 g
Protein: 21 g
Sodium: 687 mg
Fiber: 1 g
Carbohydrates: 12 g
Sugar: 5 g

65. Carrot Ginger Soup

Preparation Time: 20 minutes
Cooking Time: 21 minutes
Servings: 4
Ingredients:

- 1 tablespoon avocado oil
- 1 large yellow onion, peeled and chopped
- 1 pound carrots, peeled and chopped
- 1 tablespoon fresh peeled and minced ginger
- 1-1/2 teaspoons salt

- 3 cups vegetable broth

Directions:

1. Add the oil to the inner pot, allowing it to heat for 1 minute.
2. Add the onion, carrots, ginger, and salt and sauté for 5 minutes. Press the Cancel button.
3. Add the broth and secure the lid and adjust the time to 15 minutes.
4. Allow the soup to cool a few minutes and then transfer to a large blender. Merge on high until smooth and then serve.

Nutrition:

Calories: 99 kcal
Fat: 4 g
Protein: 1 g
Sodium: 1,348 mg
Fiber: 4 g
Carbohydrates: 16 g
Sugar: 7 g

66. Turkey Sweet Potato Hash

Preparation Time: 10 minutes
Cooking Time: 17 minutes
Servings: 4
Ingredients:

- 1-1/2 tablespoons avocado oil
- 1 medium yellow onion, peeled and diced
- 2 cloves garlic, minced
- 1 medium sweet potato, cut into cubes (peeling not necessary)
- 1/2 pound lean ground turkey
- 1/2 teaspoon salt
- 1 teaspoon Italian seasoning blend

Directions:

1. Attach the oil and allow the oil to heat 1 minute and then add the onion and cook until softened, about 5 minutes. Attach the garlic and cook an additional 30 seconds.
2. Add the sweet potato, turkey, salt, and Italian seasoning and cook for another 5 minutes.

Nutrition:

Calories: 172 kcal
Fat: 9 g
Protein: 12 g
Sodium: 348 mg
Fiber: 1 g
Carbohydrates: 10 g
Sugar: 3 g

67. Turkey Taco Lettuce Boats

Preparation Time: 10 minutes
Cooking Time: 24 minutes
Servings: 4
Ingredients:

- 1 tablespoon avocado oil
- 1 medium onion
- 2 large carrots
- 2 medium stalks celery
- 2 cloves garlic, minced
- 1 pound lean ground turkey
- 1 teaspoon chili powder
- 1 teaspoon paprika
- 1 teaspoon cumin
- 1/2 teaspoon salt
- 1/4 teaspoon black pepper
- 1 cup chipotle salsa
- 12 large romaine leaves
- 1 medium avocado, peeled, pitted, and sliced

Directions:

1. Add the oil. Set the oil to heat for 1 minute and then add the onion, carrots, celery, and garlic. Cook until softened, about 5 minutes.
2. Add the turkey and cook until brown for about 3 minutes.
3. Attach the chili powder, paprika, cumin, salt, pepper, and salsa and stir to combine.
4. To serve, set a portion of the taco meat into a romaine lettuce leaf and then top with sliced avocado.

Nutrition:

Calories: 339 kcal

Fat: 18 g
Protein: 27 g
Sodium: 900 mg
Fiber: 8 g
Carbohydrates: 18 g
Sugar: 8 g

68. Turkey and Greens Meatloaf

Preparation Time: 15 minutes
Cooking Time: 25 minutes
Servings: 4
Ingredients:

- 1 tablespoon avocado oil
- 1 small onion, peeled and diced
- cloves garlic, minced
- 3 cups mixed baby greens, finely chopped
- 1 pound lean ground turkey
- 1/4 cup almond flour
- 1 large egg
- 3/4 teaspoon salt
- 1/2 teaspoon black pepper

Directions:

1. Add the oil to the inner pot. Press the Sauté button and heat the oil for 1 minute.
2. Attach the onion and sauté until softened, 3 minutes. Add the garlic and greens and sauté for 1 more minute. Press the Cancel button.
3. In a medium bowl, combine the turkey, flour, egg, salt, and pepper.
4. Add the onion and greens mixture to the turkey mixture and stir to combine.
5. Rinse out the inner pot and then add 2 cups of water.
6. Make an aluminium foil sling by folding a large piece of foil in half and bending the edges upward.
7. Form the turkey mixture into a rectangular loaf and place it on the aluminium foil sling. Place the sling onto the steam rack with handles, and lower it into the inner pot.
8. Carefully remove the meatloaf from the inner pot and allow it to rest for 10 minutes before slicing to serve.

Nutrition:
Calories: 271 kcal
Fat: 17 g
Protein: 25 g
Sodium: 406 mg
Fiber: 2 g
Carbohydrates: 5 g
Sugar: 1 g

69. Simple Italian Seasoned Turkey Breast

Preparation Time: 10 minutes
Cooking Time: 18 minutes
Servings: 4
Ingredients:

- 11/2 pounds boneless, skinless turkey breast
- 2 tablespoons avocado oil, divided
- 1 teaspoon sweet paprika
- 1 teaspoon Italian seasoning blend
- 1/2 teaspoon kosher salt
- 1/2 teaspoon thyme
- 1/4 teaspoon garlic salt
- 1/4 teaspoon black pepper

Directions:

1. Dry the turkey breast with a towel. Cut the turkey breast in half to fit in your Instant Pot.
2. Brush both sides of the turkey breast with 1 tablespoon oil.
3. In a small bowl, mix together the paprika, Italian seasoning, kosher salt, thyme, garlic salt, and

pepper. Massage this mixture onto both sides of the turkey breast.

4. Press the Sauté button and heat the remaining 1 tablespoon oil in the inner pot for 2 minutes. Add the turkey breast and sear it on both sides, about 3 minutes per side. Press the Cancel button.

5. Remove the turkey from the inner pot and place it on a plate. Add 1 cup water to the inner pot and use a spatula to scrape up any stuck brown bits. Place the steam rack in the pot and the turkey breast on top of it.

Nutrition:
Calories: 248 kcal
Fat: 9 g
Protein: 40 g
Sodium: 568 mg
Fiber: 0 g
Carbohydrates: 0 g
Sugar: 0 g

70. Spiced Chicken and Vegetables

Preparation Time: 15 minutes
Cooking Time: 15 minutes
Servings: 4
Ingredients:

- 1 teaspoon dried thyme
- 1/4 teaspoon ground ginger
- 1/4 teaspoon ground allspice
- 1 teaspoon kosher salt
- 1/2 teaspoon black pepper
- 2 large bone-in chicken breasts
- 1/2 cup chicken stock
- 2 medium onions, peeled and cut in fourths
- 4 medium carrots

Directions:

1. In a small bowl, mix together the thyme, ginger, allspice, salt, and pepper.
2. Use half of the spice mixture to season the chicken breasts.
3. Pour the chicken stock into the inner pot and then add the chicken breasts.
4. Place the onions and carrots on top of the chicken and sprinkle them with the rest of the seasoning blend.
5. Remove the chicken and the vegetables and serve alone or with rice or lentils.

Nutrition:
Calories: 337 kcal
Fat: 5 g
Protein: 56 g
Sodium: 755 mg
Fiber: 3 g
Carbohydrates: 12 g
Sugar: 5 g

71. Lemon Garlic Turkey Breast

Preparation Time: 10 minutes
Cooking Time: 17 minutes
Servings: 4
Ingredients:

- 1 (11/2-pound) boneless, skinless turkey breast
- 2 tablespoons avocado oil, divided
- Zest from 1/2 large lemon
- 1/2 medium shallot, peeled and minced
- 1 large clove garlic, minced
- 1/2 teaspoon kosher salt
- 1/4 teaspoon black pepper

Directions:

1. Dry the turkey breast with a towel. Cut the turkey breast in half to fit in your Instant Pot.
2. Brush both sides of turkey breast with 1 tablespoon oil.
3. In a small bowl, mix together the lemon zest, shallot, garlic, salt, and pepper. Massage this mixture onto both sides of the turkey breast.
4. Press the Sauté button and heat the remaining 1 tablespoon oil in the inner pot for 2 minutes. Add the turkey breast and sear it on both

sides, about 3 minutes per side. Press the Cancel button.

5. Remove the turkey from the inner pot and place it on a plate. Add 1 cup water to the inner pot and use a spatula to scrape up any stuck brown bits. Place the steam rack in the pot and the turkey breast on top of it.

6. Slice and serve.

Nutrition:

Calories: 250 kcal

Fat: 9 g

Protein: 40 g

Sodium: 445 mg

Fiber: 0 g

Carbohydrates: 1 g

Sugar: 0 g

72. Home-style Chicken and Vegetables

Preparation Time: 5 minutes

Cooking Time: 15 minutes

Servings: 4

Ingredients:

- 2 large bone-in chicken breasts
- 1 teaspoon kosher salt, divided
- 1/2 teaspoon black pepper, divided
- 1/2 cup chicken stock
- 6 large carrots
- 8 medium whole new potatoes

Directions:

1. Flavor the chicken breasts with 1/2 teaspoon salt and 1/4 teaspoon pepper.
2. Pour the stock into the pot.
3. Add chicken breasts and place the carrots and potatoes on top of the chicken.
4. Season with the rest of the salt and pepper.
5. Transfer to the plates to serve and spoon the juices on top.

Nutrition:

Calories: 398 kcal

Fat: 5 g

Protein: 58 g

Sodium: 822 mg

Fiber: 5 g

73. Chicken Tenders with Honey Mustard Sauce

Preparation Time: 5 minutes

Cooking Time: 7 minutes

Servings: 4

Ingredients:

- 1 pound chicken tenders
- 1 tablespoon fresh thyme leaves
- 1/2 teaspoon salt
- 1/4 teaspoon black pepper
- 1 tablespoon avocado oil
- 1 cup chicken stock
- 1/4 cup Dijon mustard
- 1/4 cup raw honey

Directions:

1. Dry the chicken tenders with a towel and then season them with thyme, salt, and pepper.
2. Attach the oil and let it heat for 2 minutes. Add the chicken tenders and seer them until brown on both sides, about 1 minute per side. Press the Cancel button.
3. Remove the chicken tenders and set them aside. Add the stock to the pot. Use a spoon to scrape up any small bits from the bottom of the pot.
4. Set the steam rack in the inner pot and place the chicken tenders directly on the rack.
5. While the chicken is cooking, set the honey mustard sauce.

6. In a bowl, combine the Dijon mustard and honey and stir to combine.
7. Serve the chicken tenders with the honey mustard sauce.

Nutrition:
Calories: 223 kcal
Fat: 5 g
Protein: 22 g
Sodium: 778 mg
Fiber: 0 g
Carbohydrates: 19 g
Sugar: 18 g

74. Chicken Breasts with Cabbage and Mushrooms

Preparation Time: 10 minutes
Cooking Time: 18 minutes
Servings: 4
Ingredients:

- 2 tablespoons avocado oil
- 1 pound sliced Baby Bella mushrooms
- 1-1/2 teaspoons salt, divided
- 2 cloves garlic, minced
- 8 cups chopped green cabbage
- 11/2 teaspoons dried thyme
- 1/2 cup chicken stock
- 1-1/2 pounds boneless, skinless chicken breasts

Directions:
1. Add the oil. Allow it to heat for 1 minute. Attach the mushrooms and 1/4 teaspoon salt and sauté until they have cooked down and released their liquid, about 10 minutes.
2. Add the garlic and sauté for another 30 seconds. Press the Cancel button.
3. Add the cabbage, 1/4 teaspoon salt, thyme, and stock to the inner pot and stir to combine.
4. Dry the chicken breasts and sprinkle both sides with the remaining salt. Place on top of the cabbage mixture.
5. Transfer to plates and spoon the juices on top.

Nutrition:
Calories: 337 kcal
Fat: 10 g
Protein: 44 g
Sodium: 1,023 mg
Fiber: 4 g
Carbohydrates: 14 g
Sugar: 2 g

75. Coconut Lime Chicken and Rice

Preparation Time: 5 minutes
Cooking Time: 5 minutes
Servings: 4
Ingredients:

- 1 cup jasmine rice
- 1 can unsweetened full-fat coconut milk
- 1/2 cup chicken stock
- 1-1/4 pounds boneless, skinless chicken breasts
- 1 teaspoon salt
- 1/2 teaspoon ground cumin
- 1/4 teaspoon ground ginger
- Juice from 1 medium lime
- 1/2 cup cilantro leaves and stems

Directions:
1. Place the rice, coconut milk, stock, chicken, salt, cumin, and ginger in the inner pot and stir to combine.
2. Stir in the lime juice and spoon into four bowls. Top each bowl with an equal amount of cilantro and serve.

Nutrition:
Calories: 527 kcal
Fat: 22 g
Protein: 38 g
Sodium: 702 mg
Fiber: 1 g
Carbohydrates: 38 g
Sugar: 1 g

76. Chicken and Veggie Casserole

Preparation Time: 5 minutes
Cooking Time: 5 minutes
Servings: 4
Ingredients:

- 1/3 cup Dijon mustard
- 1/3 cup organic honey
- 1 teaspoon dried basil
- 1/4 teaspoon ground turmeric
- 1 teaspoon dried basil, crushed
- Salt and freshly ground black pepper
- 13/4 pound chicken breasts
- 1 cup fresh white mushrooms, sliced
- 1/2 head broccoli

Directions:

1. Warmth the oven to 350 degrees F. Lightly, grease a baking dish.
2. In a bowl, merge together all ingredients except chicken, mushrooms and broccoli.
3. Set chicken in prepared baking dish and top with mushroom slices.
4. Place broccoli florets around chicken evenly.
5. Pour 1 / 2 of honey mixture over chicken and broccoli evenly.
6. Bake for approximately twenty minutes.
7. Now, coat the chicken with remaining sauce and bake for approximately 10 minutes.

Nutrition:
Calories: 248 kcal
Fat: 9 g
Protein: 40 g
Sodium: 568 mg
Fiber: 0 g
Carbohydrates: 0 g
Sugar: 0 g

77. Chicken Meatloaf with Veggies

Preparation Time: 20 minutes
Cooking Time: 60 minutes
Servings: 4
Ingredients:
For Meatloaf:

- 1/2 cup cooked chickpeas
- 2 egg whites
- 21/2 teaspoons poultry seasoning
- Salt and freshly ground black pepper
- 10-ounce lean ground chicken
- 1 cup red bell pepper, seeded and minced
- 1 cup celery stalk, minced
- 1/3 cup steel-cut oats
- 1 cup tomato puree, divided
- 2 tablespoons dried onion flakes, crushed
- 1 tablespoon prepared mustard

For Veggies:

- 2 pounds summer squash, sliced
- 16-ounce frozen Brussels sprouts
- 2 tablespoons extra-virgin extra virgin olive oil
- Salt and freshly ground black pepper

Directions:

1. Warmth the oven to 350 degrees F. Grease a 9x5-inch loaf pan. In a mixer, add chickpeas, egg whites, poultry seasoning, salt and black pepper and pulse till smooth.

2. Transfer a combination in a large bowl. Add chicken, veggies oats, 1/2 cup of tomato puree and onion flakes and mix till well combined. 5. Transfer the amalgamation into prepared loaf pan evenly.
3. With both hands, press, down the amalgamation slightly. In another bowl mix together mustard and remaining tomato puree. Place the mustard mixture over loaf pan evenly.
4. Bake approximately 1-11/4 hours or till desired doneness. Meanwhile in a big pan of water, arrange a steamer basket. Bring to a boil and set summer time squash I steamer basket.
5. Cover and steam approximately 10-12 minutes. Drain well and aside.
6. Now, prepare the Brussels sprouts according to package's directions. In a big bowl, add veggies, oil, salt and black pepper and toss to coat well.
7. Serve the meatloaf with veggies.

Nutrition:
Calories: 337 kcal
Fat: 5 g
Protein: 56 g
Sodium: 755 mg
Fiber: 3 g
Carbohydrates: 12 g
Sugar: 5 g

78. Roasted Chicken with Veggies and Orange

Preparation Time: 20 minutes
Cooking Time: 60 minutes
Servings: 2
Ingredients:

- 1 teaspoon ground ginger
- 1/2 teaspoon ground cumin
- 1/2 teaspoon ground coriander
- 1 teaspoon paprika
- Salt and freshly ground black pepper
- 1 (3 1/2-4-pound) whole chicken
- 1 unpeeled orange, cut into 8 wedges
- 2 medium carrots, peeled and cut 1nto 2-inch pieces
- 2 medium sweet potatoes, peeled and cut into 1/2-inch wedges
- 1/2 cup water

Directions:

1. Preheat the oven to 450 degrees F.
2. In a little bowl, mix together the spices.
3. Rub the chicken with spice mixture evenly.
4. Arrange the chicken in a substantial Dutch oven and put orange, carrot and sweet potato pieces around it.
5. Add water and cover the pan tightly.
6. Roast for around 30 minutes.
7. Uncover and roast for about half an hour.

Nutrition:
Calories: 216
Protein: 8.83 g
Fat: 11.48 g
Carbs: 21.86 g

79. Roasted Chicken Drumsticks

Preparation Time: 15 minutes
Cooking Time: 50 minutes
Servings: 2
Ingredients:

- 1 medium onion, chopped
- 1-2 tablespoons fresh turmeric, chopped
- 1-2 tablespoons fresh ginger, chopped
- 2 lemongrass stalks (bottom third), peeled and chopped
- 1-2 jalapeños, seeded and chopped
- 1 teaspoon fresh lime zest, grated
- 1 tablespoon curry powder
- 11/4 cups unswee10ed coconut milk
- 3 tablespoons fresh lime juice
- 1 tablespoon coconut aminos
- 1 tablespoon fish sauce • 3-4 pound chicken kegs
- Chopped fresh cilantro, for garnishing

Directions:

1. In a blender, add all ingredients except chicken legs and pulse till smooth.
2. Transfer a combination in a large baking dish.
3. Add chicken and coat with marinade generously.
4. Cover and refrigerate to marinade approximately 12 hours.
5. Remove chicken from refrigerator and in room temperature approximately 25-half an hour before cooking.
6. Preheat the oven to 350 degrees F.
7. Uncover the baking dish and roast or about 50 minutes.

Nutrition
Calories 200
Carbohydrates 31g
Cholesterol 93mg
Total Fat 4g
Protein 10g

Fiber 2g
Sodium 288mg
Sugar 10g

80. Grilled Chicken Breast

Preparation Time: 15 minutes
Cooking Time: 20 minutes
Servings: 2
Ingredients:

- 2 scallions, chopped
- 1 (1-inch) piece fresh ginger, minced
- 2 minced garlic cloves
- 1 cup fresh pineapple juice
- 1/4 cup coconut aminos
- 1/4 cup extra-virgin organic olive oil
- 1 teaspoon ground cinnamon
- 1 teaspoon ground cumin
- 1 teaspoon ground turmeric
- Salt, to taste
- 4 skinless, boneless chicken breasts

Directions:

1. In a big ziploc bag add all ingredients and seal it.
2. Shake the bag to coat the chicken with marinade well.
3. Refrigerate to marinade for about twenty or so minutes to an hour.
4. Preheat the grill to medium-high heat. Grease the grill grate.
5. Place the chicken pieces on grill and grill for about 10 min per side.

Nutrition
Calories 200
Carbohydrates 31g
Cholesterol 93mg
Total Fat 4g
Protein 10g
Fiber 2g
Sodium 288mg

81. Ground Turkey with Veggies

Preparation Time: 15 minutes
Cooking Time: 12 minutes
Servings: 2
Ingredients:

- 1 tablespoon sesame oil
- 1 tablespoon coconut oil
- 1 pound lean ground turkey
- 2 tablespoons fresh ginger, minced
- 2 minced garlic cloves
- 1 (16-ounce) bag vegetable mix (broccoli, carrot, cabbage, kale and Brussels sprouts)
- 1/4 cup coconut aminos
- 2 tablespoons balsamic vinegar

Directions:

1. In a big skillet heat both oils on medium-high heat.
2. Add turkey, ginger and garlic and cook approximately 5-6 minutes.
3. Add vegetable mix and cook approximately 4-5 minutes.
4. Stir in coconut aminos and vinegar and cook for about 1 minute.
5. Serve hot.

Nutrition:
Calories: 99 kcal
Fat: 4 g
Protein: 1 g
Sodium: 1,348 mg
Fiber: 4 g
Carbohydrates: 16 g
Sugar: 7 g

82. Ground Turkey with Peas and Potato

Preparation Time: 15 minutes
Cooking Time: 35 minutes
Servings: 4
Ingredients:

- 3-4 tablespoons coconut oil
- 1 pound lean ground turkey
- 1-2 fresh red chiles, chopped
- 1 onion, chopped • Salt, to taste
- 2 minced garlic cloves
- 1 (1-inch) piece fresh ginger, grated finely
- 1 tablespoon curry powder
- 1 teaspoon ground coriander
- 1 teaspoon ground cumin
- 1 teaspoon ground turmeric
- 2 large Yukon gold potatoes
- 1/2 cup water
- 1 cup fresh peas, shelled
- 2-4 plum tomatoes, chopped
- 1/2 cup fresh cilantro, chopped

Directions:

1. In a substantial pan, heat oil on medium-high heat.
2. Attach turkey and cook for about 4-5 minutes. Add chiles and onion and cook for about 4-5 minutes. Add garlic and ginger and cook approximately 1-2 minutes.
3. Stir in spices, potatoes and water and convey to your boil Reduce the warmth to medium-low.
4. Simmer, covered approximately 15-twenty or so minutes.
5. Add peas and tomatoes and cook for about 2-3 minutes. Serve using the garnishing of cilantro.

Nutrition
Calories 546
Carbohydrates 41g
Cholesterol 31mg
Total Fat 38g
Protein 10g
Sugar 6g
Fiber 5g
Sodium 535mg

83. Turkey and Veggies Chili

Preparation Time: 1 hour
Cooking Time: 35 minutes
Servings: 8
Ingredients:

- 3 tablespoons essential olive oil, divided
- 11/2 pound lean ground turkey
- 2 tablespoons tomato paste
- 1 teaspoon dried oregano, crushed
- 1 teaspoon ground coriander
- 1 teaspoon ground cumin
- 1/2 teaspoon ground cinnamon
- 1/2 teaspoon ground turmeric
- 11/2 cups chicken broth
- 3 cups cooked sprouted beans trio
- 1/2 cup mild salsa
- 2 carrots, peeled and chopped
- 1 (141/2-ounce) can crushed tomatoes
- 1 medium onion, chopped
- 2 garlic cloves, chopped finely
- 3 medium zucchinis, chopped
- 1 cup cheddar cheese
- 4 scallions, chopped

Directions:

1. In a sizable pan, heat 1 tablespoon of oil on medium-high heat. Add turkey and with the spoon, plunge into pieces. Add tomato paste, oregano and spices and cook for about 4-5 minutes.
2. Add broth and provide to a boil, Reduce the temperature to medium and simmer for around 5 minutes. Add beans trio, salsa, carrots and tomatoes and simmer for abbot 10 minutes.
3. Meanwhile in a substantial skillet, heat remaining oil on medium-high heat. Add onion and garlic and sauté for about 5 minutes. Add zucchini

and cook for approximately 5 minutes, stirring occasionally.

4. Transfer the zucchini mixture within the chili mixture and transfer the warmth to low. 11. Simmer for around quarter-hour.

Nutrition:

Calories: 44 kcal

Fat: 1 g

Protein: 7 g

Sodium: 312 mg

Fiber: 0 g

Carbohydrates: 0 g

Sugar: 0 g

84. Roasted Whole Turkey

Preparation Time: 20 minutes

Cooking Time: 3 hours and 35 minutes

Servings: 8

Ingredients:

For Turkey Marinade:

- 1 (2-inch) piece fresh ginger, grated finely
- 3 large garlic cloves, crushed
- 1 green chili, chopped finely
- 1 teaspoon fresh lemon zest, grated finely
- 5-ounce plain Greek yogurt
- 3 tablespoons tomato puree
- 2 tablespoons fresh lemon juice
- 1 tablespoon ground cumin
- 11/2 tablespoons garam masala
- 2 teaspoons ground turmeric
- For Turkey:
- 1 (9-pound) whole turkey, giblets and neck removed
- Salt and freshly ground black pepper
- 1 garlic cloves, halved
- 1 lime, halved
- 1/2 of lemon

Directions:

1. In a bowl, merge together all marinade ingredients. With a fork, pierce the turkey completely.
2. In a sizable baking dish, put the turkey. Rub the turkey with marinade mixture evenly.
3. Refrigerate to marinate for overnight. Remove from refrigerator and make aside approximately a half-hour before serving. Preheat the oven to 390 degrees F.
4. Sprinkle turkey with salt and black pepper evenly and stuff the cavity with garlic, lime and lemon. 9. Arrange the turkey in a big roasting pan and roast for approximately a half-hour.
5. Now, reduce the temperature of oven to 350 degrees F.
6. Roast for around 3 hours. (if skin becomes brown during roasting, then cover with foil paper)

Nutrition

Calories 734

Carbohydrates 37g

Cholesterol 115mg

Total Fat 54g

Protein 25g

Sugar 3g

Fiber 5g

85. Duck with Bok Choy

Preparation Time: 15 minutes

Cooking Time: 12 minutes

Servings: 6

Ingredients:

- 2 tablespoons coconut oil
- 1 onion, sliced thinly
- 2 teaspoons fresh ginger, grated finely
- 2 minced garlic cloves
- 1 tablespoon fresh orange zest, grated finely
- 1/4 cup chicken broth

- 2/3 cup fresh orange juice
- 1 roasted duck, meat picked
- 3 pound bokchoy leaves
- 1 orange, peeled, seeded and segmented

Directions:

1. In a sizable skillet, melt coconut oil on medium heat. Attach onion, ginger and garlic and sauté for around 3 minutes. Add ginger and garlic and sauté for about 1-2 minutes.
2. Stir in orange zest, broth and orange juice.
3. Add duck meat and cook for around 3 minutes.
4. Transfer the meat pieces in a plate. Add bokchoy and cook for about 3-4 minutes.
5. Divide bokchoy mixture in serving plates and top with duck meat.
6. Serve with the garnishing of orange segments.

Nutrition:
Calories: 290
Fat: 4 g
Fiber: 6 g
Carbs: 8 g
Protein: 14 g

86. Beef with Mushroom and Broccoli

Preparation Time: 60 minutes
Cooking Time: 12 minutes
Servings: 4
Ingredients:
For Beef Marinade

- 1 garlic clove, minced
- 1 piece fresh ginger, minced
- Salt and freshly ground black pepper
- 3 tablespoons white wine vinegar
- 3/4 cup beef broth
- 1 pound flank steak, trimmed and sliced into thin strips

For Vegetables:

- 2 tablespoons coconut oil
- 2 garlic cloves
- 3 cups broccoli rabe
- 4-ounce shiitake mushrooms
- 8-ounce cremini mushrooms

Directions:

1. For marinade in a substantial bowl, mix together all ingredients except beef. Add beef and coat with marinade generously. Refrigerate to marinate for around quarter-hour.
2. In a substantial skillet, warmth oil on medium-high heat.
3. Detach beef from bowl, reserving the marinade.
4. Attach beef and garlic and cook for about 3-4 minutes or till browned.
5. In exactly the same skillet, add reserved marinade, broccoli and mushrooms and cook for approximately 3-4 minutes.
6. Set in beef and cook for about 3-4 minutes.

Nutrition
Calories 200
Carbohydrates 31g
Cholesterol 93mg
Total Fat 4g
Protein 10g
Fiber 2g

87. Beef with Zucchini Noodles

Preparation Time: 15 minutes
Cooking Time: 9 minutes
Servings: 4
Ingredients:

- 1 teaspoon fresh ginger, grated
- 2 medium garlic cloves, minced
- 1/4 cup coconut aminos
- 2 tablespoons fresh lime juice
- 11/2 pound NY strip steak, trimmed and sliced thinly
- 2 medium zucchinis, spiralized with Blade C
- Salt, to taste
- 3 tablespoons essential olive oil
- 2 medium scallions, sliced

- 1 teaspoon red pepper flakes, crushed
- 2 tablespoons fresh cilantro, chopped

Directions:

1. In a big bowl, merge together ginger, garlic, coconut aminos and lime juice. Add beef and coat with marinade generously. Refrigerate to marinate approximately 10 minutes.
2. Set zucchini noodles over a large paper towel and sprinkle with salt.
3. Keep aside for around 10 minutes.
4. In a big skillet, warmth oil on medium-high heat. Attach scallion and red pepper flakes and sauté for about 1 minute. Attach beef with marinade and stir fry for around 3-4 minutes or till browned. Add zucchini and cook for approximately 3-4 minutes.
5. Serve hot.

Nutrition
Calories 1366
Carbohydrates 166g
Cholesterol 6mg
Total Fat 67g
Protein 59g
Fiber 41g

88. Spiced Ground Beef

Preparation Time: 10 minutes
Cooking Time: 22 minutes
Servings: 5
Ingredients:

- 2 tablespoons coconut oil
- 2 whole cloves
- 2 whole cardamoms
- 1 (2-inch) piece cinnamon stick
- 2 bay leaves
- 1 teaspoon cumin seeds
- 2 onions, chopped
- Salt, to taste
- 1/2 tablespoon garlic paste
- 1/2 tablespoon fresh ginger paste
- 1 pound lean ground beef
- 11/2 teaspoons fennel seeds powder
- 1 teaspoon ground cumin
- 11/2 teaspoons red chili powder
- 1/8 teaspoon ground turmeric
- Freshly ground black pepper, to taste
- 1 cup coconut milk
- 1/4 cup water
- 1/4 cup fresh cilantro, chopped

Directions:

1. In a sizable pan, warmth oil on medium heat. Attach cloves, cardamoms, cinnamon stick, bay leaves and cumin seeds and sauté for about 20-a few seconds. Add onion and 2 pinches of salt and sauté for about 3-4 minutes. Attach garlic-ginger paste and sauté for about 2 minutes.
2. Attach beef and cook for about 4-5 minutes, entering pieces using the spoon. Secure and cook approximately 5 minutes. Stir in spices and cook, stirring for approximately 2-21/2 minutes.
3. Set in coconut milk and water and cook for about 7-8 minutes. Flavor with salt and take away from heat.
4. Serve hot using the garnishing of cilantro.

Nutrition:
Calories: 216
Protein: 8.83 g
Fat: 11.48 g
Carbs: 21.86 g

89. Ground Beef with Veggies

Preparation Time: 60 minutes
Cooking Time: 22 minutes
Servings: 4
Ingredients:

- 1-2 tablespoons coconut oil
- 1 red onion,
- 2 red jalapeño peppers
- 2 minced garlic cloves
- 1 pound lean ground beef
- 1 small head broccoli, chopped
- 1/2 of head cauliflower,
- 3 carrots, peeled and
- 3 celery ribs
- Chopped fresh thyme, to taste
- Dried sage, to taste
- Ground turmeric, to taste
- Salt and freshly ground black pepper

Directions:

1. In a large skillet, dissolve coconut oil on medium heat.
2. Attach onion, jalapeño peppers and garlic and sauté for about 5 minutes.
3. Attach beef and cook for around 4-5 minutes, entering pieces using the spoon.
4. Add remaining ingredients and cook, stirring occasionally for about 8-10 min.
5. Serve hot.

Nutrition
Calories: 141
Cholesterol: 50 mg
Carbohydrates: 6 g
Fat: 1 g
Sugar: 3 g
Fiber: 2 g

90. Ground Beef with Greens and Tomatoes

Preparation Time: 15 minutes
Cooking Time: 15 minutes
Servings: 4
Ingredients:

- 1 tbsp. organic olive oil
- 1/2 of white onion, chopped
- 2 garlic cloves, chopped finely
- 1 jalapeño pepper, chopped finely
- 1 pound lean ground beef
- 1 teaspoon ground coriander
- 1 teaspoon ground cumin
- 1/2 teaspoon ground turmeric
- 1/2 teaspoon ground ginger
- 1/2 teaspoon ground cinnamon
- 1/2 teaspoon ground fennel seeds
- Salt and freshly ground black pepper
- 8 fresh cherry tomatoes, quartered
- 8 collard greens leaves, stemmed and chopped
- 1 teaspoon fresh lemon juice

Directions:

1. In a big skillet, warmth oil on medium heat.
2. Add onion and sauté for approximately 4 minutes.
3. Attach garlic and jalapeño pepper and sauté for approximately 1 minute.
4. Attach beef and spices and cook approximately 6 minutes breaking into pieces while using spoon.
5. Set in tomatoes and greens and cook, stirring gently for about 4 minutes.
6. Whisk in lemon juice and take away from heat.

Nutrition:
Calories: 444
Fat: 15 g
Carbs: 20 g
Fiber: 2 g
Protein: 37 g

Chapter 4. Vegetables

91. Spicy Three Beans Chili

Preparation Time: 15 minutes
Cooking Time: 1 hour
Servings: 6
Ingredients:
For spice Mixture:

- 1 teaspoon dried oregano, crushed
- 1 tablespoon red chili powder
- 1 tablespoon red pepper flakes, crushed
- 2 teaspoons ground cumin
- 1 teaspoon ground turmeric
- 1 teaspoon onion powder
- 1 teaspoon garlic powder
- 1 teaspoon paprika
- Salt and freshly ground black pepper

For Chili:

- 2 tablespoons olive oil
- 1 red bell pepper, seeded and chopped
- 1 green bell pepper, seeded and chopped
- 3 large celery stalks, chopped
- 1 scallion, chopped
- 3 garlic cloves, minced
- 1 (28-ounce) can salt-free diced tomatoes
- 4 cups water
- 1 can kidney beans, rinsed and drained
- 1 can cannellini beans, rinsed and drained
- 1 (8-ounce) can black beans, rinsed and drained
- 1 jalapeño pepper, seeded and chopped

Directions:

1. For spice mixture in a bowl, mix together all ingredients. Keep aside.
2. In a large pan, warmth oil on medium heat.
3. Attach bell peppers, celery, scallion and garlic and sauté for about 8-10 minutes.
4. Attach spice mixture, tomatoes and water and bring to a boil.
5. Simmer for about 20 minutes.
6. Stir in beans and jalapeño pepper and simmer for about 30 minutes.
7. Serve hot.

Nutrition:
Calories: 302
Fat: 6g
Sat Fat: 1g
Carbohydrates: 50g
Fiber: 15g
Protein: 16g
Sodium: 488mg

92. Chickpeas Chili

Preparation Time: 15 minutes
Cooking Time: 25 minutes
Servings: 4
Ingredients:

- 2 teaspoons olive oil
- 1 cup onion, chopped
- 1/2 cup carrot, peeled and chopped
- 3/4 cup celery, chopped
- 1 teaspoon garlic, minced
- 2 teaspoons ground cumin
- 1 teaspoon ground ginger

- 1/2 teaspoon ground turmeric
- 1/8 teaspoon ground cinnamon
- 2 teaspoons paprika
- 1/8 teaspoon red chili powder
- Salt and freshly ground black pepper
- 2 (151/2-ounce) cans chickpeas, rinsed and drained
- 1 (141/2-ounce) can salt-free diced tomatoes
- 2 tablespoons salt-free tomato paste
- 11/2 cups water
- 1 tablespoon fresh lemon juice
- 2 tablespoons fresh cilantro, chopped

Directions:

1. In a large pan, warmth oil on medium heat.
2. Attach onion, carrot, celery and garlic and sauté for about 5 minutes.
3. Add spices and sauté for about 1 minute.
4. Add chickpeas, tomatoes, tomato paste and water and bring to a boil.
5. Set the heat to low and simmer, covered for about 20 minutes.
6. Stir in lemon juice and cilantro and remove from heat.
7. Serve hot.

Nutrition:

Calories: 215

Fat: 5g

Sat Fat: 4g

Carbohydrates: 33g

Fiber: 8g

Protein: 7g

Sodium: 534mg

93. Lentils Chili

Preparation Time: 15 minutes

Cooking Time: 2 hours 6 minutes

Servings: 8

Ingredients:

- 2 teaspoons olive oil
- 1 large onion, chopped
- 3 medium carrot, peeled and chopped
- 4 celery stalks, chopped
- 2 minced garlic cloves
- 2 tablespoons tomato paste
- 11/2 tablespoons ground coriander
- 11/2 tablespoons ground cumin
- 11/2 teaspoons ground turmeric
- 1 teaspoon chipotle chili powder
- Salt and freshly ground black pepper
- 1 pound lentils, rinsed
- 8 cups vegetable broth
- 1 cup fresh spinach, chopped
- 1/4 cup fresh mint leaves, chopped
- 1/4 cup fresh cilantro, chopped

Directions:

1. In a large pan, warmth oil on medium heat.
2. Attach onion, carrot and celery and sauté for about 5 minutes.
3. Add garlic, tomato paste and spices and sauté for about 1 minute.
4. Add lentils and broth and bring to a boil.
5. Set the heat to low and simmer.
6. Stir in spinach and remove from heat.
7. Serve hot with the garnishing of mint and cilantro.

Nutrition:

Calories: 216

Protein: 8.83 g

Fat: 11.48 g

Carbs: 21.86 g

94. Grains Chili

Preparation Time: 15 minutes

Cooking Time: 51 minutes

Servings: 12

Ingredients:

- 2 tablespoons olive oil
- 2 shallots, chopped
- 1 large yellow onion, chopped
- 1 tablespoon fresh ginger, grated finely
- 8 garlic cloves, minced
- 1 teaspoon ground cumin

- 3 tablespoons red chili powder
- Salt and freshly ground black pepper
- 1 (28-ounce) can crushed tomatoes
- 1 canned chipotle pepper, minced
- 1 Serrano pepper, seeded and chopped finely
- 2/3 cup bulgur wheat
- 2/3 cup pearl barley
- 21/4 cups mixed lentils (green, black, brown), rinsed
- 11/2 cups canned chickpeas
- 3 scallions, chopped

Directions:

1. In a large pan warmth oil on medium heat.
2. Attach shallot and onion and sauté for about 4-5 minutes.
3. Add ginger, garlic, cumin and chili powder and sauté for about 1 minute.
4. Stir in tomatoes, both peppers and broth.
5. Stir in the remaining ingredients except the scallion and bring to a boil.
6. Set the heat to low and simmer till desired thickness of the chili.
7. Serve hot with the topping of scallion.

Nutrition

Calories 200

Carbohydrates 31g

Cholesterol 93mg

Total Fat 4g

Protein 10g

Fiber 2g

95. Red Lentils Curry

Preparation Time: 15 minutes

Cooking Time: 23 minutes

Servings: 8

Ingredients:

- 2 cups red lentils, rinsed
- 1 tbsp. olive oil
- 1 large onion, chopped
- 1 teaspoon fresh ginger, minced
- 1 teaspoon garlic, minced
- 2 tablespoons curry paste
- 1 tablespoon curry powder
- 1 teaspoon ground cumin
- 1 teaspoon ground turmeric
- 1 teaspoon red chili powder
- Salt and freshly ground black pepper
- 1 (141/4-ounce) can tomato puree

Directions:

1. In a large pan of water, add lentils and bring to a boil on high heat. Se the heat to medium-low and simmer, covered for about 15-20 minutes. Drain well.
2. Meanwhile in a large skillet, heat oil on medium heat. Add onion and sauté for about 20 minutes.
3. Meanwhile in a bowl, mix together all remaining ingredients except tomato puree. Add spice mixture into the skillet with onions on medium-high heat. Sauté for about 1-2 minutes. Stir in tomato puree and cook for about 1 minute.
4. Transfer the mixture into the pan with the lentils and stir to combine. Serve hot.

Nutrition:
Calories: 192
Fat: 6g
Sat Fat: 3g
Carbohydrates: 35g
Fiber: 13g
Sugar: 6g
Protein: 11g
Sodium: 572mg

96. Red Lentils with Spinach

Preparation Time: 15 minutes
Cooking Time: 30 minutes
Servings: 4
Ingredients:

- 31/2 cups water
- 11/2 cups red lentils, soaked for 20 minutes and drained
- 1/2 teaspoon red chili powder
- 1/2 teaspoon ground turmeric
- Salt, to taste
- 1 pound fresh spinach, chopped
- 2 tablespoons coconut oil
- 1 onion, chopped
- 1 teaspoon mustard seeds
- 1 teaspoon ground cumin
- 1/2 cup coconut milk
- 1 teaspoon garam masala

Directions:

1. In a large pan, add water, lentils, red chili powder, turmeric and salt and bring to a boil on high heat.
2. Set the heat to low and simmer, covered for about 15 minutes.
3. Stir in spinach and simmer for about 5 minutes.
4. In a frying pan, dissolve coconut oil on medium heat.
5. Add onion, mustard seeds and cumin and sauté for about 4-5 minutes.
6. Set the onion mixture into the pan with the lentils and stir to combine.
7. Stir in coconut milk and garam masala and simmer for about 3-4 minutes.
8. Serve hot.

Nutrition:
Calories: 362
Fat: 14g
Sat Fat: 2g
Carbohydrates: 49g
Fiber: 13g
Sugar: 5g
Protein: 21g
Sodium: 693mg

97. Vegetarian Balls in Gravy

Preparation Time: 20 minutes
Cooking Time: 25 minutes
Servings: 4-6
Ingredients:
For Balls:

- 1 cup cooked chickpeas
- 1 cup cooked red kidney beans
- 1/2 cup cooked quinoa
- Salt and freshly ground black pepper
- 2 tablespoons black beans flour
- 1 medium onion, chopped
- 2 garlic cloves, chopped
- 1/4 cup fresh cilantro, chopped
- 1 teaspoon cumin seeds
- Pinch of baking soda
- 1 tablespoon fresh lemon juice
- 2 teaspoons olive oil

For Gravy:

- 1 teaspoon olive oil
- 1 teaspoon cumin seeds
- 1 medium onion, chopped finely
- 1 (1-inch) piece fresh ginger, grated finely
- 2 tomatoes, chopped finely
- 2 green chilies, chopped finely

- 1/2 teaspoon garam masala
- 1/2 teaspoon ground turmeric
- 1/2 teaspoon red chili powder
- Salt, to taste
- 2 cups water
- 1/4 cup fresh cilantro, chopped

Directions:

1. For balls in a food processor, add all ingredients except oil and pulse till a coarse meal forms. Transfer the mixture into a bowl. Cover the bowl with a foil paper and refrigerate for at least 1 hour. Remove the mixture from refrigerator and make equal sized balls.
2. In a nonstick skillet, warmth oil on medium heat. Cook the balls for about 2-3 minutes or till golden brown from all sides.
3. For gravy in a nonstick pan, heat oil on medium heat. Add cumin seeds and sauté for about 1 minute. Add onion and sauté for about 6-7 minutes. Stir in ginger, tomatoes, green chilies and spices and cook for about 1-2 minutes.
4. Add water and bring to a boil.
5. Set the heat to low and simmer, covered for about 10 minutes.
6. Carefully, place the balls in the gravy and cook for about 1-2 minutes. Sprinkle with cilantro and serve.

98. Quinoa with Veggies

Preparation Time: 15 minutes

Cooking Time: 35 minutes

Servings: 3

Ingredients:

- 2 tablespoons olive oil
- 1 small onion, minced
- 2 carrots, peeled and sliced
- 1 celery stalk, chopped
- 1 garlic clove, minced
- 1/2 cup uncooked quinoa, rinsed
- 1 teaspoon ground turmeric
- 1/4 teaspoon dried basil, crushed
- Salt, to taste
- 1 cup vegetable broth
- 1 teaspoon fresh lime juice

Directions:

1. In a pan, warmth oil on medium heat.
2. Attach onion, carrot, celery and garlic and sauté for about t minutes.
3. Stir in remaining ingredients except lime juice and bring to a gentle simmer.
4. Set the heat to low and simmer, covered for about 25-30 minutes or till all the liquid is absorbed.
5. Stir in lime juice and serve.

Nutrition:

Calories: 227

Fat: 11g

Sat Fat: 5g

Carbohydrates: 23g

Fiber: 32

Sugar: 2g

Protein: 2g

Sodium: 195mg

99. Quinoa with Asparagus

Preparation Time: 15 minutes
Cooking Time: 18 minutes
Servings: 4
Ingredients:

- 1 pound fresh asparagus, trimmed
- 2 teaspoons coconut oil
- 1/2 of onion, chopped
- 2 minced garlic cloves
- 1 cup cooked red quinoa
- 1 tablespoon ground turmeric
- 1/2 cup reduced-sodium vegetable broth
- 1/2 cup nutritional yeast
- 1 tablespoon fresh lemon juice

Directions:

1. Set a pan of boiling water, cook the asparagus for about 2-3 minutes.
2. Drain well and rinse under cold water.
3. In a large skillet, dissolve coconut oil on medium heat.
4. Attach onion and garlic and sauté for about 5 minutes.
5. Stir in quinoa, turmeric and broth and cook for about 5-6 minutes.
6. Stir in nutritional yeast, lemon juice and asparagus and cook for about 3-4 minutes.

Nutrition:
Calories: 166
Fat: 2g
Sat Fat: 1g
Carbohydrates: 21g
Fiber: 9g
Sugar: 9g
Protein: 13g
Sodium: 37mg

100. Quinoa and Beans with Veggies

Preparation Time: 20 minutes
Cooking Time: 26 minutes
Servings: 6
Ingredients:

- 2 cups water
- 1 cup dry quinoa
- 2 tablespoons coconut oil
- 1 medium onion, chopped
- 4 garlic cloves, chopped finely
- 2 tablespoons curry powder
- 1/2 teaspoon ground turmeric
- Cayenne pepper, to taste
- Salt, to taste
- 2 cups broccoli, chopped
- 1 cup fresh kale, trimmed and chopped
- 1 cup green peas, shelled
- 1 red bell pepper, seeded and chopped
- 2 cups canned kidney beans
- 2 tablespoons fresh lime juice

Directions:

1. In a pan, attach water and bring to a boil on high heat. Add quinoa and reduce the heat to low. Simmer for about 10-15 minutes or till all the liquid is absorbed.
2. In a large skillet, dissolve coconut oil on medium heart. Add onion, garlic, curry powder, turmeric and salt and sauté for about 4-5 minutes. Add the vegetables and cook for about 5-6 minutes. Stir in quinoa and beans. Drizzle with lime juice and serve.

Nutrition:
Calories: 290
Fat: 4 g
Fiber: 6 g
Carbs: 8 g
Protein: 14 g

101. Coconut Brown Rice

Preparation Time: 15 minutes
Cooking Time: 1 hour
Servings: 14
Ingredients:

- 12 cups water
- 1 tablespoon dried turmeric
- 2 pound brown rice
- 2 (131/2-ounce) cans lite coconut milk
- 2 (131/2-ounce) cans coconut milk
- 1 tablespoon fresh ginger, minced
- 11/2 teaspoons fresh lemon zest, grated finely
- 4 dried bay leaves
- Salt and freshly ground black pepper
- Chopped cashews, for garnishing
- Chopped fresh cilantro, for garnishing

Directions:

1. In a small bowl, add water and turmeric and beat till well combined.
2. In a large pan, add turmeric water and remaining ingredients except cashews and stir well.
3. Bring to a boil on high heat.
4. Set the heat to medium and simmer, stirring occasionally for about 30-35 minutes.
5. Set the heat to low and simmer, covered for about 20-25 minutes.
6. Remove bay leaf before serving.
7. Garnish with cashews and cilantro and serve.

Nutrition:
Calories: 184
Fat: 2g
Carbohydrates: 27g
Fiber: 7g
Sugar: 9g
Protein: 2g
Sodium: 76mg

102. Brown Rice and Cherries Pilaf

Preparation Time: 20 minutes
Cooking Time: 35 minutes
Servings: 8
Ingredients:

- 1 (14-ounce) can low-sodium vegetable broth
- 1/3 cup water
- 1 cup brown basmati rice
- 1 tablespoon curry powder
- 1/2 teaspoon ground turmeric
- Pinch of saffron threads, crumbled
- 1/3 cup fresh lemon juice
- 3 tablespoons olive oil
- 3 tablespoons raw honey
- 1 tablespoon fresh ginger, minced
- 1 tablespoon fresh orange zest, grated finely
- Salt, to taste
- 3/4 cup celery stalk, chopped
- 1/2 cup scallion, chopped, divided
- 3/4 cup dried cherries, chopped roughly
- 1 cup fresh dark sweet cherries, pitted and chopped
- 3/4 cup unsalted mixed nuts

Directions:

1. In a pan, mix together broth, water, rice, curry powder, turmeric and saffron and bring to a boil on medium-high heat.
2. Set the heat to low and simmer, covered for about 35 minutes.
3. Detach from heat and keep aside, covered for about 5 minutes.
4. With a fork, fluff the rice.
5. In a large glass bowl, merge together lemon juice, oil, honey, ginger, orange zest and salt.
6. Stir in cooked rice, celery, 1/4 cup of scallion and dried cherries.
7. Serve immediately with the topping of fresh cherries, nuts and remaining scallion.

Nutrition:
Calories: 288
Fat: 12g
Sat Fat: 1g
Carbohydrates: 41g
Fiber: 5g
Protein: 6g
Sodium: 125mg

103. Brown Rice Casserole

Preparation Time: 15 minutes
Cooking Time: 1 hour
Servings: 2
Ingredients:

- 1 teaspoon extra-virgin olive oil
- 1 red onion, sliced thinly
- 11/2 teaspoons ground turmeric
- 9-ounce brown mushrooms, sliced
- 1 teaspoon raisins
- 1/2 cup brown rice, rinsed
- 11/4 cups vegetable broth
- 1/4 cup fresh cilantro, chopped
- 1/2 tablespoons pine nuts, toasted
- 1 tablespoon fresh lemon juice
- Salt and freshly ground black pepper

Directions:

1. Preheat the oven to 400 degrees F.
2. In an ovenproof casserole, heat oil on medium heat.
3. Add onion and turmeric and sauté for about 3 minutes.
4. Attach mushrooms and stir fry for about 2 minutes.
5. Stir in raisins, rice and broth and transfer into oven.
6. Bake for about 45-55 minutes or till desired doneness.
7. Just before serving, stir in remaining ingredients.

Nutrition:
Calories: 201

Fat: 5g
Sat Fat: 6g
Carbohydrates: 37g
Fiber: 5g
Sugar: 18g
Protein: 7g
Sodium: 384mg

104. Rice, Lentils and Veggie Casserole

Preparation Time: 20 minutes
Cooking Time: 1 hour 36 minutes
Servings: 10
Ingredients:

- 33/4 cups water, divided
- 1/2 cup brown lentils, rinsed
- 1/2 cup wild rice, rinsed
- 1 tbsp. olive oil
- 1/2 of medium onion, chopped
- 1 cup button mushrooms, sliced
- 1 cup tomato sauce
- 1 (10-ounce) package frozen spinach, thawed and squeezed
- 1 (16-ounce) package frozen peas, thawed
- 2 minced garlic cloves
- 1 tablespoon dried oregano, crushed
- 1 teaspoon smoked paprika
- 1/2 teaspoon ground turmeric
- 1/4 cup nutritional yeast

For Sauce

- 11/4 cups unsweetened almond milk
- 1 cup unsalted cashews
- 1 teaspoon coconut aminos
- 1/2 teaspoon dried garlic

Directions:

1. In a pan, add 3 1/2 cups of water, lentils and rice and bring to a boil. Set the heat to low and simmer, covered for about 35 minutes. Remove from heat and keep aside to cool.
2. Warmth the oven to 350 degrees F. Grease a 13x9-inch casserole dish. In a large skillet, heat 2 tablespoons of water on high heat. Add onion and sauté for about 2-3 minutes. Attach mushrooms and cook for about 2 minutes.
3. Add remaining 2 tablespoons of water and remaining ingredients except nutritional yeast and cook for about 1 minute. Remove from heat and mix with rice mixture. Transfer the mixture into prepared casserole dish evenly.
4. In a blender, attach all sauce ingredients and pulse till smooth. Spread the sauce over the rice mixture evenly and stir to combine well. Top with nutritional yeast evenly.
5. Bake for about 45 minutes.

Nutrition:
Calories: 223 kcal
Fat: 5 g
Protein: 22 g
Sodium: 778 mg
Fiber: 0 g
Carbohydrates: 19 g
Sugar: 18 g

105. Herbed Bulgur Pilaf

Preparation Time: 20 minutes
Cooking Time: 35 minutes
Servings: 6
Ingredients:

- 2 tablespoons extra-virgin olive oil
- 2 cups onion, chopped
- 1 garlic clove, minced
- 11/2 cups medium bulgur
- 1/2 teaspoon ground cumin
- 1/2 teaspoon ground turmeric
- 11/2 cups carrot, peeled and chopped
- 2 teaspoons fresh ginger, grated finely
- Salt, to taste
- 2 cups vegetable broth
- 3 tablespoons fresh lemon juice
- 1/4 cup fresh parsley, chopped
- 1/4 cup fresh mint leaves, chopped
- 1/4 cup fresh dill, chopped
- 1/2 cup walnuts, toasted and chopped

Directions:

1. In a large deep skillet, warmth oil on medium-low heat. Add onion and cook, stirring occasionally for about 12-18 minutes. Add garlic and sauté fir about 1 minute.
2. Add bulgur, cumin and turmeric and stir fry for about 1 minute. Add carrot, ginger, salt and broth and bring to a boil, stirring occasionally. Simmer, covered for about 15 minutes.
3. Detach from heat and keep aside, covered for about 5 minutes.
4. Stir in lemon juice and fresh herbs and serve with the garnishing of walnuts.

Nutrition:
Calories: 277
Fat: 12g
Sat Fat: 1g
Carbohydrates: 39g
Fiber: 10g
Protein: 7g
Sodium: 507mg

106. Biryani

Preparation Time: 15 minutes
Cooking Time: 15 minutes
Servings: 6
Ingredients

- Black pepper as desired
- Sea salt as desired
- Garam masala .5 tsp.
- Coconut oil 1 tsp.
- Shelled peas 1 c
- Water 5 c
- Coriander .5 tsp. ground
- Chili powder 1 tsp.
- Turmeric 5 tsp.
- Carrots 2 quartered
- Potatoes 2 quartered
- Bay leaves 2 torn
- Cumin seeds .5 tsp.
- Onion 1 sliced thin
- Vegetable oil 3 T
- White rice long grain 2 c

Directions

1. Add the rice to a large pot and cover it with three to four inches of water before allowing it to soak for about 20 minutes. Drain and set aside.
2. Add the oil to your pressure cooker and set it over medium heat. Add in the onion, bay leaves, and cumin seeds and let everything cook about 5 minutes until the onion is nearly see through.
3. Mix in the carrots and potatoes and let them cook an additional 5 minutes and the potatoes have begun to brown. Add in the coriander, turmeric and chili powder and let everything cook 1 additional minute.
4. Attach the rice to the pressure cooker and ensure it is well covered in the boil before adding in the peas and water. Mix in the garam masala, oil, and salt before sealing the cooker and turning it to high pressure. Let everything cook for 5 minutes before removing from heat.
5. Allow the pressure to naturally release and fluff the rice with a fork prior to serving.

Nutrition:
Calories: 9 kcal
Fat: 0 g
Protein: 0 g
Sodium: 585 mg
Fiber: 0 g
Carbohydrates: 2 g

107. Greek Mixed Roasted Vegetables

Preparation Time: 15 minutes
Cooking Time: 45 minutes
Servings: 4
Ingredients-
Vegetables

- 1 eggplant peeled and diced .75-inch
- Black pepper as desired
- Kosher sea salt as desired
- Extra virgin olive oil 2 T
- Garlic 2 cloves minced
- Onion 1 peeled, diced 1-inch
- Bell pepper 2 red, yellow, diced, 1-inch

Dressing

- Coconut oil .25 c
- Lemon juice .3 c squeezed fresh
- Black pepper as desired
- Kosher sea salt as desired
- Basil 15 leaves
- Scallions 4 minced

Directions

1. Ensure your oven is heated to 425F.
2. One a sheet pan, combine the garlic, onion, yellow bell pepper, red bell pepper, and eggplant before seasoning using the pepper, salt, and coconut oil.
3. Add the pan to the oven and let it cook for 40 minutes, using a spatula to flip everything after 20 minutes.
4. As the vegetables are cooking, combine the pepper, salt, coconut oil, and lemon juice together in a small bowl, add the results to the vegetables as soon as they are ready.
5. Let the pan cool completely before adding in the basil, feta, and scallions. Season prior to serving.

Nutrition:
Calories: 337 kcal
Fat: 5 g
Protein: 56 g
Sodium: 755 mg
Fiber: 3 g
Carbohydrates: 12 g
Sugar: 5 g

108. Autumn Roasted Green Beans

Preparation Time: 15 minutes
Cooking Time: 30 minutes
Servings: 4
Ingredients

- Walnuts .5 c toasted
- Cranberries .5 c dried
- Black pepper as desired
- Kosher sea salt as desired
- Lemon juice 2 tsp.

- Lemon zest 1 tsp.
- Sugar .25 tsp.
- Coconut oil 2 T
- Garlic 4 cloves, quartered and peeled
- Green beans 2 lbs. stems trimmed

Directions

1. Preheat your oven to 350F and crack and smash the walnuts into chunks.
2. Spread the walnuts onto a baking sheet and toast them for 10 minutes.
3. Increase the temperature on the oven to 450F.
4. Cover a baking sheet with a rim using aluminum foil.
5. In a mixing bowl, combine the sugar, pepper, salt and coconut oil before coating the garlic and green beans thoroughly.
6. Place the beans onto a baking sheet and spread them out to ensure they cook well. Place the sheet into the oven and let the beans bake for 15 minutes, before stirring with a spatula and roasting another 10 minutes.
7. Mix in the lemon juice, pepper and salt prior to serving.

Nutrition
Calories 200
Carbohydrates 31g
Cholesterol 93mg
Total Fat 4g
Protein 10g
Fiber 2g

109. Roasted Summer Squash

Preparation Time: 5 minutes
Cooking Time: 30 minutes
Servings: 4
Ingredients

- Zucchini 3
- Yellow squash 3
- Kosher salt 5 Tbs.
- Black pepper .5 Tbs.
- Coconut oil 2 Tbs.

Directions

1. Ensure your oven is heated to 400F
2. Peel vegetables and cut into.25 inch thick slices.
3. Assemble vegetables on a baking sheet or pan and drizzle coconut oil on top. Sprinkle with seasoning as desired
4. Bake at 400F for 30 minutes.

Nutrition:
Calories: 288
Fat: 12g
Sat Fat: 1g
Carbohydrates: 41g
Fiber: 5g
Protein: 6g
Sodium: 125mg

110. Savory Baked Acorn Squash

Preparation Time: 5 minutes
Cooking Time: 30 minutes
Servings: 4
Ingredients

- Acorn squash 1
- Kosher salt as desired
- Black pepper as desired
- Coconut oil 2 tsp.
- Smoked paprika as desired

Directions

1. Ensure your oven is heated to 425F.
2. Cut acorn squash in half lengthwise, then cut halves into quarters lengthwise. Scoop out seeds and discard.
3. Place the squash on baking sheet and drizzle coconut oil over the top of each quarter. Scatter

with the smoked paprika, salt, and pepper and bake in the oven for 30 minutes.

Nutrition:

Calories: 9 kcal

Fat: 0 g

Protein: 0 g

Sodium: 585 mg

Fiber: 0 g

Carbohydrates: 2 g

111. Roasted Brussels Sprouts

Preparation Time: 5 minutes

Cooking Time: 15 minutes

Servings: 4

Ingredients

- Sea salt .25 tsp.
- Black pepper .25 tsp.
- Brussel sprouts .75lbs. sliced in half length-wise
- Coconut oil 5 Tbs..

Directions

1. Ensure your oven is heated to 400F. Divide Brussels sprouts in half and place in a medium-sized bowl. Drizzle the coconut oil over the Brussels sprouts and then toss with the sea salt and black pepper until evenly coated.
2. Set Brussels sprouts onto a baking sheet and make sure they are evenly spaced so that they will roast easily.
3. Place the sheet in the oven and let it cook approximately 10 minutes before stirring well and returning it to the oven for 10 minutes more. Season as desired They will keep in the fridge for 3-4 days, or in the freezer for 2-3 months.

Nutrition:

Calories: 223 kcal

Fat: 5 g

Protein: 22 g

Sodium: 778 mg

Fiber: 0 g

Carbohydrates: 19 g

Sugar: 18 g

112. Roasted Rosemary Potatoes

Preparation Time: 10 minutes

Cooking Time: 25 minutes

Servings: 6

Ingredients

- Garlic 1 head
- Rosemary 3 sprigs
- Thyme 3 sprigs
- Baby potatoes 20 oz.
- Parsley 2 T chopped
- Sea salt as desired
- Black pepper as desired
- Coconut oil 2 T

Directions

1. Ensure your oven is heated to 450F.
2. Separate garlic cloves and remove the papery skin holding them together, but do not peel.
3. Add the rosemary, thyme, baby potatoes, parsley, garlic, and coconut oil together in a large bowl, coating well.
4. Add the results to a jelly roll pan that has been lined with tinfoil before topping with pepper and salt. Set the pan in the oven and let the potatoes bake approximately 25 minutes, stirring at the 12-minute mark.
5. Season with additional pepper and salt prior to serving.

Nutrition:

Calories: 337 kcal

Fat: 5 g

Protein: 56 g

Sodium: 755 mg
Fiber: 3 g
Carbohydrates: 12 g
Sugar: 5 g

113. Sweet Potato Wedges

Preparation Time: 10 minutes
Cooking Time: 30 minutes
Servings: 6
Ingredients

- Salt 1 tsp.
- Cracked black pepper 1 tsp.
- Garlic powder .5 tsp.
- Sweet potatoes 4 medium, peeled, each cut into 6 wedges
- Rosemary 1 T chopped, fresh
- Coconut oil 2 T

Directions

1. Preheat oven to 450F.
2. In a mixing bowl, combine the coconut oil, rosemary, sweet potatoes, garlic powder, black pepper, and salt together and ensure the potatoes are coated well.
3. Add the results in a single layer to a large roasting pan before placing the pan in the oven and letting the potatoes bake for 20 minutes. Turn the dish at this point before baking another 10 minutes.

Nutrition:
Calories: 288
Fat: 12g
Sat Fat: 1g
Carbohydrates: 41g
Fiber: 5g
Protein: 6g
Sodium: 125mg

114. Best Lentil Curry

Preparation Time: 10 min
Cooking Time: 30 minutes
Servings: 4
Ingredients

- Vegetable broth 4 c low sodium
- Red lentil 1 c
- Potato 10 oz. peeled and made into pieces that are 1 inch each
- Carrot 8 oz. chopped
- Curry powder 1 T
- Scallions 8 separated, sliced
- Garlic 2 cloves chopped
- Ginger 2 T chopped
- Coconut oil 3 T

Directions

1. •Add the oil to a saucepan before placing it on the stove on top of a burner set to a high/medium heat.
2. •Add in the scallion whites, garlic and ginger and let them soften for 2 minutes.
3. •Mix in the curry powder as well as pepper and salt, as desired, broth, lentils, potato, and carrots before letting everything boil. Set down the heat and let everything simmer for 15 minutes, stirring regularly.
4. •Top with scallion greens prior to serving.

Nutrition
Calories 200
Carbohydrates 31g
Cholesterol 93mg
Total Fat 4g
Protein 10g
Fiber 2g

115. Chana Masala

Preparation Time: 5 minutes
Cooking Time: 25 minutes
Servings: 4
Ingredients

- Curry powder 1 tsp.
- Chickpeas 32 oz. rinsed, drained
- Garlic 2 cloves minced
- Onion 1 large, chopped
- Extra virgin olive oil 1 T
- Cilantro .25 c
- Kosher sea salt as desired
- Lemon juice 1 T
- Tomatoes 2 chopped
- Ginger 2 tsp. grated
- Turmeric .5 tsp.

Directions

1. Add the oil to a skillet before placing it on a burner set to a medium/high heat. Add in the onion and let it sauté until it has become translucent and soft. Mix in the garlic and let it cook for 3 minutes.
2. Add in the curry powder, chickpeas, coconut oil, lemon juice, tomatoes, ginger and turmeric along with.25 c of water. Let the mixture simmer before cooking it for 10 minutes, stirring on occasion. The end result should have a stew-like consistency but not be runny.
3. Season using salt and top with cilantro prior to serving.

Nutrition:
Calories: 290
Fat: 4 g
Fiber: 6 g
Carbs: 8 g
Protein: 14 g

116. Zucchini Noodle Pasta with Avocado Pesto

Preparation Time: 30 minutes
Cooking Time: 15 minutes
Servings: 8
Ingredients

- Zucchinis 6 spiralized
- Cold pressed oil of choice 1 T

Pesto

- Pine nuts .25 c
- Avocados 2 cubed
- Parsley .25 c leaves
- Basil 1 c leaves
- Garlic 3 cloves
- Lemon juice 1 lemon
- Cold pressed oil of choice 3 T
- Salt as desired
- Pepper as desired

Directions

1. Set your zucchini and set aside on paper towels.
2. In a food processor, add in all ingredients for the avocado pesto except the oil. Set on low until desired consistency is reached.
3. Slowly add in coconut oil until creamy and emulsified.
4. Heat 1 T and your zucchini noodles cook for 4 min.
5. Take your zucchini noodles and coat with avocado pesto.

Nutrition
Calories 200
Carbohydrates 31g
Cholesterol 93mg
Total Fat 4g
Protein 10g
Fiber 2g

117. Thai Soup

Preparation Time: 30 minutes
Cooking Time: 15 minutes
Servings: 9
Ingredients

- Spiralized Zucchinis 2 medium
- Minced Garlic Cloves 2 total
- Thin Sliced Red Pepper 1 total
- Diced Jalapeno 1 total
- Lime 1 cut into 8 wedges
- Thin Sliced Onion 5 total
- Full-Fat Coconut Milk 15oz
- Vegetable Broth 6 c
- Fresh Chopped Cilantro 5 c
- Green Curry Paste 5 T
- Coconut Oil 1 T

Directions

1. Add the coconut oil to a saucepan before adding in the onions and letting them sauté. Takes about 5 minutes.
2. Add jalapeno, curry paste, and minced garlic. Sauté for 1 minute or until just fragrant. Stir in bone broth and coconut milk, mix until thoroughly combined. Warmth until soup comes to a boil and then reduce to medium heat. Add red pepper slices, then mix.
3. Simmer soup approximately 5 minutes or until done, until chicken is cooked through. Add fresh cilantro.
4. Divide zucchini into 8 bowls and ladle soup over them. The heat of the soup will cook the zucchini noodles. If not serving all at once, store soup and zoodles separately and combine when prepared to eat, so zoodles don't become soggy.

Nutrition
Calories 734
Carbohydrates 37g
Cholesterol 115mg
Total Fat 54g
Protein 25g

118. Vegan Lasagna

Preparation Time: 10 minutes
Cooking Time: 4 hours
Servings: 8
Ingredients

- Lasagna Zoodles 6
- Vegan cheese 5 c
- Red pepper flakes .25 tsp.
- Basil .5 tsp. dried
- Oregano 1 tsp. dried
- Salt 1 tsp.
- Tomato sauce 15 oz.
- Tomato 28 oz. crushed
- Garlic 1 clove minced
- Onion 1 chopped
- Ground soy 1 lb.

Directions

1. Place a skillet on the stove on top of a burner set to a high/medium heat before adding in the garlic, onion, and soy and letting the soy brown.
2. Add in the red pepper flakes, basil, oregano, salt, tomato sauce, and crushed tomatoes and let the results simmer 5 minutes.
3. Add.3 of the total sauce from the skillet and add it to the slow cooker. Place 3 Zoodles on top of the sauce, followed by cheese mixture. Create three layers in total.
4. Secure the slow cooker and let it cook on a low heat for 6 hours.

Nutrition
Calories 1366
Carbohydrates 166g
Cholesterol 6mg
Total Fat 67g
Protein 59g
Fiber 41g

119. Caprese Zoodles

Preparation Time: 10 minutes
Cooking Time: 15 minutes
Servings: 4
Ingredients

- Zucchini 4 large
- 2 T coconut oil
- Kosher salt as desired
- Black pepper as desired
- Cherry tomatoes, 2 c halved
- Mozzarella balls 1 c quartered
- Basil leaves .25 c torn
- Balsamic vinegar 2 T

Directions

1. Place the zoodles in a serving bowl before adding in the coconut oil and tossing well. Season as desired and allow the zoodles to marinate for at least 15 minutes.
2. Mix in the basil, mozzarella, and tomatoes and toss well.
3. Top with balsamic prior to serving.

Nutrition
Calories 200
Carbohydrates 31g
Cholesterol 93mg
Total Fat 4g
Protein 10g
Fiber 2g

120. Lemon Green Beans With Almonds

Preparation Time: 10 minutes
Cooking Time: 20 minutes
Servings: 4
Ingredients

- Green beans 500 g
- Almonds 120g
- Lemon
- 3 tablespoons Extra virgin olive oil
- 4 tbsp. Beetroot leaves
- 150g Salt to taste

Directions:

1. Warmth the oven to 180 C. Toast the almonds on a baking tray for 5 minutes.
2. Add green beans and steam them for about 5 minutes until they are al dente. Emulsify olive oil and lemon juice in a bowl.
3. Add a pinch of salt. Put the green beans, almonds and beetroot leaves in a large bowl. Set the dressing over the salad and mix well. Serve immediately.

Nutrition:
Calories: 288
Fat: 12g
Sat Fat: 1g
Carbohydrates: 41g
Fiber: 5g
Protein: 6g

Chapter 5. Seafood and Fish

121. Almond Pesto Salmon

Preparation Time: 10 minutes
Cooking Time: 15 minutes
Servings: 4
Ingredients

- Garlic clove (1)
- Almonds (.25 cup)
- Olive oil (1 tbsp.)
- Lemon (.5 of 1)
- Parsley (.5 tsp.)
- Pink Himalayan salt (.5 tsp.)
- Atlantic salmon fillets (2 @ 170 g/ 6 oz. each)
- Shallot (half of 1)
- Lettuce (2 handfuls)
- Butter (2 tbsp.)

Directions:

1. Prepare the Pesto: Pulse the garlic, almonds, and oil in the food processor to make the paste. Mix in the parsley, salt, and juice of the lemon. Set to the side.
2. Use a paper towel to remove the moisture from the salmon fillets.
3. Sprinkle with a dusting of pepper and salt to your liking.
4. Cook the salmon for four to six minutes (skin side down) in a lightly greased pan. Flip it and butter the pan to baste the fish for a minute or so (rare inside).
5. Store the pesto in the fridge.
6. When the salmon is done, cool entirely. Set in the fridge overnight or freeze for later.
7. When ready to eat, just serve over some lettuce with a dollop of pesto, slivered almonds, and shallots.

Nutrition:
Total Net Carbohydrates: 6 grams
Fat Content: 47 grams
Protein: 38 grams
Calories: 610

122. Baked Coconut Shrimp

Preparation Time: 10 minutes
Cooking Time: 15 minutes
Servings: 4
Ingredients

- Medium shrimp (1 lb./42-48)
- Salt and black pepper (.5 tsp. each)
- Eggs (3 large)
- Coconut flour (3 tbsp.)
- Paprika (.25 tsp.)
- Garlic powder (.25 tsp.)
- Coconut flakes - unsweetened (2 cups)

Directions:

1. Peel, devein, and thaw the shrimp.
2. Heat the oven to 400 Fahrenheit/204° Celsius.
3. Lay a wire rack on the top of a cookie sheet and spray it with oil spray.
4. Set three bowls separately on the counter. In the first one, whisk the eggs; in the next one, place the coconut flakes. In the last one, whisk a

mixture of salt, pepper, paprika, garlic powder, and coconut flour.

5. Dip each shrimp individually into the flour mixture first, then into the egg wash, and then roll in coconut flakes. Set them on the wire rack and bake for ten minutes, turning them over after five minutes.

Nutrition:

Total Net Carbohydrates: 5 grams

Fat Content: 30 grams

Protein: 31 grams

Calories: 443

123. Broiled Dill Tilapia Parmesan

Preparation Time: 10 minutes

Cooking Time: 15 minutes

Servings: 4

Ingredients

- Tilapia fillets (5-6 oz./140-170 g each)
- Non-fat plain yogurt (2 tsp.)
- Light mayonnaise (2 tsp.)
- Parmesan cheese (.25 cup - shredded)
- Fresh dill (2-4 sprigs)
- Garlic or powder salt - divided (1 tsp.)
- Black pepper (as desired)
- Non-stick cooking spray (as needed)

Directions:

1. Set the oven to broil on high.
2. Combine the yogurt with the mayo and parmesan cheese in a mixing container. Prepare a baking tray using a layer of aluminum foil and spray it with the cooking spray.
3. Arrange the fillets on the tray - about two inches apart. Spread half of the cheese mixture over each fillet. Dust the fillets using a sprinkle of dill, garlic powder, pepper, and salt to your liking.
4. Arrange the cookie sheet about six inches below the broiler (first rack).
5. Bake for five to seven minutes. Once the cheese starts to brown, check them every 1/2 minute or so. They're ready when the fish is easily flaked.
6. Turn the broiler off. Set the tray in the oven for around five minutes.
7. Remove the tray from the oven and serve the delicious fish with your preferred side dishes.

Nutrition:

Total Net Carbohydrates: 1.4 grams

Fat Content: 8.2 grams

Protein: 48.5 grams

Calories: 272

124. Delicious Parmesan Shrimp

Preparation Time: 30 minutes

Cooking Time: 15 minutes

Servings: 2

Ingredients

- Shrimp (14 medium/26-30 per lb. count)
- Olive oil (1 tbsp.)
- Garlic (half of 1 clove)
- Light salt (2 dashes)
- Creole seasoning (.25 tsp.)
- Fresh ground pepper (2 dashes)
- Panko breadcrumbs (.125 cup or 1/8 cup)
- Shredded parmesan cheese (1 tbsp.)
- Optional: Lemon wedges
- Butter-flavored/keto-friendly cooking spray (as needed)
- Also Needed: 8x8 baking pan

Directions:

1. You can use either - fresh and thawed pre-peeled shrimp. Mince the garlic.
2. Peel and devein the shrimp and toss them into a zipper-type bag with the garlic, olive oil, salt, pepper, and creole seasoning
3. Place the bag in the fridge for 30 minutes to one hour.
4. Heat the oven at 475 Fahrenheit/246 Celsius.
5. Toss the breadcrumbs and parmesan into the baggie and gently turn to coat.

6. Arrange the shrimp in a single layer into the ungreased pan so they're not touching. Spritz the baking tray using the cooking spray.
7. Broil for approximately ten minutes until done. Serve promptly.
8. Garnish with lemon wedges as desired (add the carbs).

Nutrition:
Total Net Carbohydrates: 4.5 grams
Fat Content: 8.6 grams
Protein: 10.2 grams
Calories: 138

125. Lemon Butter Scallops

Preparation Time: 10 minutes
Cooking Time: 30 minutes
Servings: 4
Ingredients

- Butter (4 tbsp. - divided)
- Scallops (1 lb.)
- Lemon zest and juice (1 lemon)
- Pepper and salt (to your liking)

Directions:
1. Rinse the scallops under cold tap water and pat dry. Season with pepper and salt.
2. Slice the lemon in half, using for the juice and half for the zest.
3. Over the medium-high heat setting, melt two tablespoons of the butter. Toss in the scallops and prepare for five to seven minutes per side.
4. Once they're crispy, squeeze half of the freshly squeezed lemon juice over the scallops and add to a serving dish.
5. Attach the rest of the butter to the skillet and blend in the rest of the lemon juice and lemon zest. Stir it for four to five minutes or until the butter is slightly reduced.
6. The leftovers are good for up to two days if stored in an airtight container.

Nutrition:
Total Net Carbohydrates: 5 grams
Fat Content: 22.7 grams
Protein: 15.9 grams
Calories: 289

126. Lemon Garlic Mahi-Mahi Fillets

Preparation Time: 10 minutes
Cooking Time: 15 minutes
Servings: 4
Ingredients

- Butter (3 tbsp. - divided)
- Olive oil (2 tbsp. - divided)
- Mahi-mahi fillets (4 @ 4-oz./110 g each)
- Black pepper and kosher salt (as desired)
- Asparagus (1 lb.)
- Garlic (3 cloves)
- Red pepper flakes (.25 tsp.)
- Lemon (1 sliced/zest and juice)
- Freshly chopped parsley (1 tbsp. + more for garnish)

Directions:
1. Prepare a large skillet using the medium-temperature setting - adding one tablespoon each of butter and oil.
2. Arrange the fish in the pan with a dusting of salt and pepper. Cook until golden or about four to five minutes on each side. Plate it for now.
3. Add the remainder of the oil into the skillet. Toss in the asparagus with pepper and salt. Sauté until it's tender (2 to 4 min.). Transfer it to a plate.
4. Put the last two tablespoons of butter into the skillet. Mince and add the garlic, pepper flakes, lemon juice, zest, and parsley.

5. Take the pan off of the burner. Add back the fish and asparagus to the skillet and add the sauce.
6. Serve with parsley as desired.

Nutrition:
Total Net Carbohydrates: -0- grams
Fat: 13 grams
Protein: 21 grams
Calories: 200

127. Lemon Garlic Shrimp Pasta

Preparation Time: 30 minutes
Cooking Time: 15 minutes
Servings: 4
Ingredients

- Miracle Noodle Angel Hair Pasta (2 bags/as desired)
- Olive oil (2 tbsp.)
- Butter (2 tbsp.)
- Garlic (4 cloves)
- Jumbo raw shrimp (450 g/1 lb.)
- Lemon (half of 1)
- Paprika (.5 tsp.)
- Fresh basil
- Pepper and salt (as desired)

Directions:
1. Set the water from the package of noodles and wash them in cold water. Add them to a pot of boiling water for two minutes. Transfer them to a hot pot over medium heat to remove the excess liquid (dry roast). Set them to the side.
2. Using the same pan, add the oil, butter, and smashed garlic. Cook for a few minutes – not browned.
3. Divide the lemon into rounds and add them to the garlic, along with the shrimp. Saute for approximately three minutes per side. Add the noodles and spices and stir to blend the flavors.

Nutrition:
Total Net Carbohydrates: 3.5 grams
Fat Content: 21 grams
Protein: 36 grams
Calories: 360

128. Mediterranean Grilled Ahi Tuna

Preparation Time: 10 minutes
Cooking Time: 4 hours
Servings: 4
Ingredients

- Ahi Tuna Steaks (1-inch thick 4 140 g/5 oz. each Uncooked fresh or frozen-thawed)
- E-V olive oil (1 tbsp.)
- Black pepper (.25 tsp.)
- Kosher salt (.5 tsp.)
- Lemon juice (1 lemon wedge/.5 tsp.)
- Finely chopped oregano (.5 tsp.) or dried (.25 tsp.)
- Red pepper flakes (.25 tsp.) or crushed/dried (a dash)
- Fresh basil (1 tsp.) or dried (.25 tsp.)
- Garlic (1 clove)

Directions:
1. Warm an outside grill using the med-high temperature setting, or start the charcoal grill for about 1/2 hour.
2. Remove excess moisture from the steaks using paper towels and place them into a shallow dish.
3. Finely mince the garlic. Whisk the spices with oil and lemon juice. Wait for at least five minutes to blend the flavors.
4. Set the mixture on both sides of the steaks and wait another five minutes.
5. Grill the tuna steaks for two to five minutes on each side. Rare is most preferred with a slightly pink center.

Nutrition:
Total Net Carbohydrates: 0.4 grams
Fat: 5 grams
Protein: 43 grams

Calories: 229

129. Piccata Fish Cakes

Preparation Time: 30 minutes
Cooking Time: 15 minutes
Servings: 9
Ingredients
The Cakes:

- Tuna (2 cans 5 oz./140 g each)
- Sardines - packed in olive oil (2 cans 3.75 oz./110 g)
- Mayonnaise (.25 cup)
- Egg (1)
- Italian Breadcrumbs - ex. Pork King Good (.25 cup)
- Capers (2 tbsp.)
- Lemon juice (1 tbsp.)
- Calabrian Chili Powder (.5 tsp.)
- Parsley (1 tbsp.)

The Aioli:

- Mayonnaise (.5 cup)
- Capers w/brine (2 tbsp.)
- Lemon juice (1 tbsp.)
- Italian seasoning (1 tbsp.)
- Chili powder (.5 tsp.)
- Parsley (1 tbsp.)
- Garlic (1 tbsp.)
- Vinegar - red wine (1 tbsp.)

Additional Ingredients:

- Italian breadcrumbs - ex. - Pork King (1 cup)
- Ghee/Avocado oil (.33 cup)

Directions:

1. Mince the garlic. Chop the capers and parsley and set them to the side for now.
2. Drain the tuna and shred it into a bowl. Mix in the sardines with oil to the bowl and shred. Attach and mix in the remainder of the fixings. Chill it in the fridge for 15 minutes.
3. Prepare each cake into three-ounce balls. Coat with breadcrumbs. Fry them in a cast-iron skillet using the medium-temperature setting with ghee.
4. Cook for three minutes on each side. If you prefer a crispier fish cake, flatten the patties to make them thinner by pressing down on the cakes with a spatula while the first side is cooking.
5. Prepare the Aioli by combining all of the fixings in a mixing container or mason jar. Pulse with a stick blender to combine. For a chunky dressing, whisk the ingredients. You can use it for up to three weeks when stored in the fridge.
6. Serve the fish cakes over a plate of lettuce with aioli.

Nutrition:
Total Net Carbohydrates: -0- grams
Fat: 34 grams
Protein: 31 grams
Calories: 445

130. Salmon Cakes

Preparation Time: 10 minutes
Cooking Time: 4 hours
Servings: 4
Ingredients

- Wild Alaskan Pink Salmon - ex. - Bumble Bee (420 g/14.75 oz. can)
- Raw onion (1 cup + more if desired)
- Garlic powder (1 tsp.)
- Large egg (1)

- Black pepper (1 tsp.)
- Salt (as desired)
- Butter or other fat (for frying)

Directions:

1. Mix all of the fixings to form four patties.
2. Fry patties as you would a hamburger in a bit of butter for flavoring.
3. Serve with your favorite sides or in a sandwich.

Nutrition:

Total Net Carbohydrates: 3.6 grams
Fat: 10.1 grams
Protein: 23.2 grams
Calories: 195

131. Salmon with Spinach and Pesto

Preparation Time: 30 minutes
Cooking Time: 15 minutes
Servings: 4
Ingredients

- Salmon (2 lb./910 g)
- Black pepper (1 tsp.)
- Salt (.5 tsp.)
- Parmesan cheese - grated (2 oz./56 g)
- Spinach - fresh (1 lb./450 g)
- Sour cream (1 cup)
- Pesto - green or red (1 tbsp.)
- Butter (1 tbsp.)
- Suggested: 9x13/23x33-cm baking dish

Directions:

1. Warm the oven to 400 Fahrenheit/204° Celsius.
2. Grease the baking dish with lard (3 tbsp.).
3. Season the salmon with salt and pepper. Place them in the baking pan with the skin down.
4. Blend the pesto with the sour cream and parmesan cheese in a small bowl. Use the mixture to thoroughly coat the salmon.
5. Bake the fish for 20 minutes.
6. Meanwhile, fry the spinach using the medium-temperature setting in the butter. Simmer until the spinach wilts (3-5 min.).
7. Serve the spinach with the baked salmon.

Nutrition:

Total Net Carbohydrates: 3 grams
Fat: 78 grams
Protein: 45 grams
Calories: 902

132. Seafood Imperial

Preparation Time: 10 minutes
Cooking Time: 15 minutes
Servings: 5
Ingredients

- Lump crabmeat (450 g/1 lb.)
- Shrimp (230 g/.5 lb.)
- Sea scallops (.5 lb.)
- Mayonnaise (.5 cup)
- Eggs (2)
- Lemon juice (1 lemon)
- Chopped parsley (2 tbsp.)
- Sliced scallions (2 tbsp.)
- Old Bay (.5 tsp.)
- Baking powder (.5 tsp.)

Directions:

1. Cook shrimp and scallops in boiling water for about two minutes. Pour them into an ice water bath to stop the cooking process.
2. Peel the shrimp, cut into bite-size pieces, and quarter the scallops. Pick the crab meat looking for any tiny bits of shell.
3. In another container, whisk all the rest of the fixings to make the imperial sauce. Set half of the sauce over the shrimp, scallops, and crab mixture. Gently fold in to mix the ingredients.
4. Let the mixture set up for 1/2 hour in the fridge.
5. Scoop the mixture into oven-safe dishes.
6. Bake at 425° Fahrenheit or 218° Celsius until a light crust begins to form (10-12 min.).

7. Garnish the seafood with the remainder of the imperial sauce mixture and continue baking until the sauce turns golden brown (5-7 min.).

Nutrition:
Total Net Carbohydrates: -0- grams
Fat: 20 grams
Protein: 34 grams
Calories: 334

133. Sesame Ginger Salmon

Preparation Time: 30 minutes
Cooking Time: 15 minutes
Servings: 2
Ingredients

- Salmon fillet (280 g/10 oz.)
- Ginger (1 to 2 tsp.)
- White wine (2 tbsp.)
- Ketchup - sugar-free (1 tbsp.)
- Sesame oil (2 tsp.)
- Soy sauce (2 tbsp.)
- Rice vinegar (1 tbsp.)
- Fish sauce - ex. Red Boat (1 tbsp.)
- Needed: Pan with a tight-fitting top

Directions:

1. Mince the ginger beforehand. Toss each of the fixings in a container with a top - omitting the ketchup, oil, and wine for now. Marinade for about 1o to 15 minutes.
2. On the stovetop, set a skillet using the high heat temperature setting and pour in the oil. Add the fish when it's hot with the skin side facing down.
3. Brown both sides. When you flip it over, pour in the marinated juices and simmer. Arrange the fish on two dinner plates.
4. Add the wine and ketchup into the skillet and simmer for five minutes until it's reduced. Serve with your favorite side dish.

Nutrition:
Total Net Carbohydrates: 2.5 grams
Protein: 33 grams
Fat: 24 grams
Calories: 370

134. Shrimp Asparagus Noodles

Preparation Time: 10 minutes
Cooking Time: 15 minutes
Servings: 2
Ingredients

- Thick asparagus spears (450 g/1 lb.)
- Butter (2 tbsp.)
- Garlic (2 cloves)
- Zested lemon (1)
- Lemon juice (2 tsp.)
- Salt (.25 tsp.)
- Cooked shrimp (170 g/6 oz.)
- Asiago or our preference sharp grated cheese (2 tbsp.)

Directions:

1. Trim the asparagus ends and mince the garlic. Make ribbons from the asparagus with a veggie peeler.
2. Use a big skillet to melt the butter. Toss in the garlic - sauté for one to two minutes. Stir in the zest, juice, and salt.
3. Toss in the deveined shrimp and sauté for another one to two minutes until heated.
4. Toss in the noodles and sauté for three minutes.
5. Drizzle with cheese and serve.

Nutrition:
Total Net Carbohydrates: 3.3 grams
Fat: 17 grams
Protein: 23.6 grams

Calories: 253

135. Asparagus and Mixed Salad

Preparation Time: 10 minutes
Cooking Time: 15 minutes
Servings: 4
Ingredients

- Desalted cod 300 gr Metapontino
- strawberries 100 gr
- Asparagus 50 gr
- Arugula 20 gr
- Borage flowers 10 gr
- Yellow pepper 10 gr
- Fresh broad beans 20 gr
- Oil ex. Virgin of Ferrandina 100 gr
- Salt of Maldon to taste lemon 4 slices

For the Dressing

- 1 Strawberries 100 gr
- Mint 10 gr Oil
- ex. virgin of Ferrandina 50 gr
- 2 Basil 50 gr
- Oil ex. Virgin of Ferrandina 50 gr.

Directions:

1. Desalinate the cod for at least 24 hours. Slice thinly with a knife and season with extra virgin olive oil. Clean and wash the strawberries with the rest of the vegetables, cut each vegetable into a different shape.
2. The strawberry must be cut into wedges, put everything in a bowl and mix gently, thus creating the salad that will accompany the cod.

For the dressing

1. Blend strawberries, oil, and mint in a special glass. Repeat the same preparation with the basil and the oil for the second dressing.
2. Arrange the slices of cod in a shallow dish, place the salad on top and season with both dressing, then add a few slices of lemon.

Nutrition:
Calories: 201
Fat: 5g
Sat Fat: 6g
Carbohydrates: 37g
Fiber: 5g
Sugar: 18g
Protein: 7g

136. Cuttlefish Salad in Sweet and Sour Sauce

Preparation Time: 10 minutes
Cooking Time: 15 minutes
Servings: 2
Ingredients

- 550g of fresh cuttlefish
- 30g of raisins
- 20g of pine nuts
- 80g of oil
- 60g of vinegar rose grapes
- Salt to taste
- Parsley in leaves
- 1 head of radicchio

Directions:

1. Clean the cuttlefish and blanch in the water, the fins and the weave take longer. Cool and cut into julienne strips.
2. Clean the radicchio and cut it thinly.

3. In a steel bowl, mix cuttlefish, radicchio, raisins, pine nuts, vinegar, oil, salt and a teaspoon of sugar.
4. Leave to marinate and flavor. Serve in a radicchio leaf. Decorate with parsley leaves.

Nutrition
Calories 1366
Carbohydrates 166g
Cholesterol 6mg
Total Fat 67g
Protein 59g
Fiber 41g

137. Coronel Carpaccio And Dried Cherry Tomatoes

Preparation Time: 10 minutes
Cooking Time: 15 minutes
Servings: 4
Ingredients

- Coronel (stockfish fillet) 500gr.
- Dried cherry tomatoes
- Black olives
- Extra virgin olive oil
- White pepper
- Capers "lacrimelle"
- Pomegranate or wild strawberries (depending on the season)

Directions:

1. The main component of this dish, but like all dishes, in addition to the freshness of any ingredients, consists of the high quality of the stockfish and in the right salting, otherwise you risk upsetting the simplicity of the dish itself.
2. The Coronel is peeled and the dish is mounted as if the gills were so many petals. It is a kind of tapenade of olives and cherry tomatoes and rests harmoniously on the coronel petals, together with the desalted capers.
3. Decorate the whole with pomegranate grains or with the pickled strawberries.

Nutrition:
Calories: 248 kcal
Fat: 9 g
Protein: 40 g
Sodium: 568 mg
Fiber: 0 g
Carbohydrates: 0 g
Sugar: 0 g

138. Flag Fish Roll with Smoked Provola

Preparation Time: 10 minutes
Cooking Time: 30 minutes
Servings: 4
Ingredients

- 2 kg of fish flag
- 150g smoked cheese
- bread grated
- extra-virgin olive oil
- salt, capers, garlic, and parsley
- Fillet the flag fish, making 30 cm fillets each.

Directions

1. Compose the filling with a smoked provola nut, grated bread, capers, and minced garlic, wrap the fillets on themselves, bread them in the breadcrumbs. Bake for about 5-7 minutes.
2. Pour a drizzle of extra virgin olive oil over the fillets and decorate with parsley leaves.

Nutrition
Calories 1366
Carbohydrates 166g
Cholesterol 6mg
Total Fat 67g
Protein 59g
Fiber 41g

139. Spaghetti Marinara

Preparation Time: 30 minutes
Cooking Time: 15 minutes
Servings: 4
Ingredients

- Fresh or peeled San Marzano tomato 500 gr
- Black Gaeta olives 50 gr
- Desalinated capers 50 gr
- Extra virgin olive oil 80 gr
- Garlic 1 clove
- Oregano, salt to taste
- Spaghetti 350 gr

Directions:

1. Let the garlic go in the oil.
2. Remove it blond. Add the tomatoes, olives, capers and cook for a quarter of an hour.
3. Taste for salt.
4. Lower the pasta and remove it al dente. Attach the spaghetti to the sauce and add plenty of oregano.
5. Jump on the plate.

Nutrition:
Calories: 398 kcal
Fat: 5 g
Protein: 58 g
Sodium: 822 mg
Fiber: 5

140. Vermicelli with Cuttlefish Ink

Preparation Time: 10 minutes
Cooking Time: 30 minutes
Servings: 4
Ingredients

- 320 grams of linguine, vermicelli or spaghetti, even spaghettoni
- 3 very fresh squid ink pockets
- 250 gr. of cuttlefish
- 1 clove of garlic
- A very fresh lemon
- Extra virgin olive oil
- Fresh mint leaves

Directions:

1. Clean the cuttlefish well, peel them and carefully collect the black bags and set them aside. Brown in a large pan 8 tablespoons of extra virgin olive oil with the whole garlic and just crushed, pour the well-dried cuttlefish cut into small pieces and fry for 2 minutes.
2. At the same time, cook the vermicelli or spaghetti or even spaghetti in abundant salted water.
3. In a bowl, mix the black cuttlefish pasta in very little cooking water and pour it into the pan with the cuttlefish sauce, mixing well.
4. Strain the pasta al dente with a couple of minutes in advance and finish cooking by sautéing it in the pan with the dressing of the cuttlefish and the black, 2 drops of lemon each and, if necessary, add the pasta cooking water.

Nutrition:
Calories: 99 kcal
Fat: 4 g
Protein: 1 g
Sodium: 1,348 mg
Fiber: 4 g
Carbohydrates: 16 g
Sugar: 7 g

141. Ribbons with Thalli and Tuna

Preparation Time: 10 minutes
Cooking Time: 30 minutes
Servings: 2
Ingredients

- 200g of ribbons
- 200g of zucchini seeds
- 100g of tuna Callipo reserve gold
- 2 tablespoon of olive oil
- pepper
- garlic

Directions

1. While the pasta is cooking, take the thalli clean and cut into strips, pass them quickly in boiling water.
2. On a frying pan, make the garlic sweat and then remove it.
3. Add the thalli, Turn quickly.
4. Drain the pasta al dente and then add it to the thalli
5. Another minute then turn off the heat, add the tuna and turn over pepper.
6. You can serve.

Nutrition:
Calories: 337 kcal
Fat: 5 g
Protein: 56 g
Sodium: 755 mg
Fiber: 3 g
Carbohydrates: 12 g

142. Bluefin Tuna at the Two Sesame

Preparation Time: 30 minutes
Cooking Time: 15 minutes
Servings: 2
Ingredients

- 180gr of Sicilian red tuna
- 30 gr white and black sesame mix
- 25 grams of avocado
- 25gr of eggplant
- 15g candied ginger
- 20 gr soy sauce
- Salt and pepper and oil to taste

Directions:

1. Fillet and clean the red tuna, cut it into fillets and pass it in sesame. Blanch the fillets over high heat and cut into medallions. Separately cut the aubergines into strips, fry them and marinate them in soy.
2. Cut the red onions and cook in the sweet and sour sauce, peel the avocado and merge it with a little oil and a dash of lemon
3. Place the tuna medallions on the plate and add the aubergines, the candied ginger, the avocado quenelles, the micro-salad and the chervil and season with the soy sauce.

Nutrition:
Calories: 2049
Protein: 56.21 g
Fat: 143.36 g
Carbs: 139.98 g

143. Escarole and Cetara Anchovies Pie with Raisins and Pine Nuts

Preparation Time: 10 minutes
Cooking Time: 30 minutes
Servings: 8
Ingredients

- 2 heads of endive
- extra virgin olive oil
- 24 black olives from Gaeta
- 20 capers from Pantelleria desalinated
- 50 grams of stale bread
- 10 grams of pine nuts
- 20 grams of raisins

- 16 fillets of desalted anchovies
- 2 cloves of Italian garlic
- Prezzzemolo, enough
- 2 eggs.

Directions:

1. In a saucepan, put the garlic to fry with extra virgin olive oil.
2. As soon as the garlic turns blond, add the endive that you have previously washed and coarsely chopped.
3. When the endive is withered, add black olives and capers that you have carefully washed and desalted and proceed with quick-cooking.
4. Let cool and place in a container.
5. Add the bread cut into cubes and the eggs that will serve to tie it all together.
6. Take some oil molds and fill them with the endive and bake at 160 degrees for 10 minutes.
7. Apart from having put the raisins to soak and toasted the pine nuts.
8. Put the baked pie in a shallow dish, garnish with raisins and toasted pine nuts, add the salted anchovies, preferably Cetara and a sprinkling of parsley.

Nutrition

Calories 144

Carbohydrates 14g

Cholesterol 0mg

Total Fat 8g

Protein 4g

Sugar 1g

Fiber 4g

Sodium 606mg

144. Shrimp Pie

Preparation Time: 10 minutes

Cooking Time: 30 minutes

Servings: 8

Ingredients

- 250g of flour
- 200g of cold butter
- 1 teaspoon salt
- 3 tbsp. water
- 2 tbsp. olive oil
- 2 cloves garlic,
- 400g shrimp
- 1 tomato
- 2 tbsp. coconut milk
- 1 minced finger pepper
- 1/4 cup sour cream
- 2 tbsp. chopped cilantro
- 1 gem

Directions:

1. Set the flour in a bowl and add the diced butter.
2. Knead with fingertips until crumbly.
3. Attach salt and, gradually, water until it turns into dough. Secure with plastic and refrigerate for 1 hour.
4. Warnth a frying pan, sprinkle with olive oil and brown the garlic and prawns.
5. Attach the tomatoes, sauté for a couple of minutes, then add coconut milk and pepper and cook for another two minutes.

6. Flavor with salt, add the cream, turn off the heat and add the cilantro. Set aside to cool.
7. To open the dough in portions and to cover the pancakes, to stuff with the shrimp and to cover with a circle of dough.
8. Set with the yolk and bake in the preheated oven at 180 degrees for about 30 minutes or until golden brown.

Nutrition:
Calories: 248 kcal
Fat: 9 g
Protein: 40 g
Sodium: 568 mg
Fiber: 0 g
Carbohydrates: 0 g
Sugar: 0 g

145. Creamy Shrimp Oven Rice

Preparation Time: 10 minutes
Cooking Time: 30 minutes
Servings: 8
Ingredients

- 2 tbsp. olive oil
- 600g clean little shrimp
- 1 clove minced garlic
- 1 chopped seedless tomato
- 2 tbsp. tomato extract
- 1 cup canned sour cream
- salt
- Black pepper
- 1/4 cup chopped parsley
- 5 cups cooked rice
- 2 gems
- 1 jar (200g) of curd
- 1/2 cup Parmesan + 1/2 cup sprinkling

Directions:

1. Heat a skillet, sprinkle with olive oil, and brown the shrimp. Add the garlic, the chopped tomatoes, sauté for 2 minutes and add the tomato extract and then the cream, flavor with salt and pepper, turn off the heat and set aside.
2. In a bowl, combine rice, egg yolks, curd, and 1/2 cup Parmesan.
3. Cover the bottom of a previously oiled refractory with rice. Arrange the prawns, cover with parsley, and 1/2 cup Parmesan cheese.
4. Bake at 180 degrees until the cheese browned.

Nutrition:
Calories: 44 kcal
Fat: 1 g
Protein: 7 g
Sodium: 312 mg
Fiber: 0 g
Carbohydrates: 0 g
Sugar: 0 g

146. Shrimp in the Pumpkin

Preparation Time: 10 minutes
Cooking Time: 30 minutes
Servings: 8
Ingredients

- 1 large pumpkin
- 8 cloves garlic, minced
- 1 1/2 minced onion
- Black pepper to taste
- Salt to taste
- 3 tablespoons olive oil + braised olive oil
- 1kg clean, fresh shrimp
- 2 chopped tomatoes
- 1/2 cup of passata
- 1/4 bunch of coriander
- 2 seedless minced finger peppers
- 1 can of sour cream
- 1 cup of curd
- 100g grated mozzarella cheese

Directions

1. Open the pumpkin, remove the seeds. Reserve. Knead 5 cloves of garlic with 1/2 onion, black pepper, salt, and olive oil. Rub this paste inside the pumpkin, cover and bake at 180 degrees for 30 minutes.

2. Season the shrimps with salt, black pepper, and lemon juice. In a hot skillet with a drizzle of olive oil, brown the prawns, season with salt and pepper, and set aside.
3. Sauté the remaining onion, garlic and add the tomatoes and cook for 10 minutes.
4. Add the coriander, the pepper, the cream, the curd, the prawns, and correct the salt.
5. Arrange the shrimp with the sauce inside the pumpkin and mix it with the cooked pumpkin from the inside.
6. Top with grated mozzarella cheese. Bake for 20 minutes or until browned.

Nutrition:
Calories: 248 kcal
Fat: 9 g
Protein: 40 g
Sodium: 568 mg
Fiber: 0 g
Carbohydrates: 0 g
Sugar: 0 g

147. Potato Dumpling with Shrimp

Preparation Time: 10 minutes
Cooking Time: 30 minutes
Servings: 8
Ingredients

- 500g potatoes
- 1 egg
- salt
- 1 tbsp. parsley
- 2 tablespoons flour + flour for handling and breading
- 10 units of clean giant tailed shrimp
- black pepper
- 1/2 packet of chopped cilantro
- 3 tablespoons palm oil
- 4 lemon juice
- frying oil

Directions
1. Set the potato to cook for 40 minutes.
2. When very tender, detach from heat, let cool and mash potatoes already peeled.
3. Attach the egg and merge well, flavor with salt and parsley and add the flour. Set aside in the fridge for 2 hours.
4. Set small transverse cuts on the belly of the shrimp, without cutting to the end. Flavor the shrimp; salt, black pepper, chopped coriander, palm oil, and lemon juice. Leave marinating for 15 minutes.
5. Set a portion of the potato flour dough in your hands and shape around a shrimp leaving the tail out.
6. Wash flour again and fry in hot oil until golden.

Nutrition:
Calories: 223 kcal
Fat: 5 g
Protein: 22 g
Sodium: 778 mg
Fiber: 0 g
Carbohydrates: 19 g
Sugar: 18 g

148. Creamy Shrimp Cone

Preparation Time: 10 minutes
Cooking Time: 30 minutes
Servings: 8
Ingredients

- Braised olive oil
- 3 cloves minced garlic
- 400g Shrimp Sauce (clean and peeled)
- 2 tablespoons tomato paste

- 1 cup of coconut milk
- Salt to taste
- 1 minced finger pepper
- 2 tbsp. chopped cilantro
- 100g grated mozzarella cheese
- 100g of bread bran

Directions

1. In olive oil, sauté the garlic until it gives off an aroma.
2. Add the shrimp.
3. Add tomato extract, coconut milk, and reduce for 10 minutes over medium heat.
4. Season with salt, pepper, ginger, and chopped coriander.
5. Arrange in peels or ramekins, arrange portions of mozzarella cheese and portions of breadcrumbs and bake 180 degrees until browned.

Nutrition:

Calories: 302

Fat: 6g

Sat Fat: 1g

Carbohydrates: 50g

Fiber: 15g

Protein: 16g

Sodium: 488mg

Chapter 6. Side Dishes

149. Green Beans

Preparation Time: 5 minutes
Cooking Time: 10 minutes
Servings: 5
Ingredients:

- 1/2 teaspoon of red pepper flakes
- 2 tablespoons of extra-virgin olive oil
- 2 garlic cloves, minced
- 1-1/2 lbs. green beans, trimmed
- 2 tablespoons of water
- 1/2 teaspoon kosher salt

Directions:

1. Warmth oil in a skillet on medium temperature.
2. Include the pepper flake. Set to coat in the olive oil. Include the green beans. Cook for 7 minutes. Stir often.
3. The beans should be brown in some areas. Attach the salt and garlic. Cook for 1 minute, while stirring. Pour water and cover immediately.
4. Cook covered for 1 more minute.

Nutrition:
Calories 82
Carbohydrates 6 g
Total Fat 6 g
Protein 1 g
Fiber 2 g
Sugar 0 g
Sodium 230 mg

150. Roasted Carrots

Preparation Time: 10 minutes
Cooking Time: 40 minutes
Servings: 4
Ingredients:

- 1 onion, peeled and cut
- 8 carrots, peeled and cut
- 1 teaspoon thyme, chopped
- 2 tablespoons of extra-virgin olive oil
- 1/2 teaspoon rosemary, chopped
- 1/4 teaspoon ground pepper
- 1/2 teaspoon salt

Directions:

1. Preheat your oven to 425 degrees F.
2. Merge the onions and carrots by tossing in a bowl with rosemary, thyme, pepper, and salt. Spread on your baking sheet. Roast for 40 minutes.

Nutrition:
Calories 126
Carbohydrates 16 g
Total Fat 6 g
Protein 2 g
Fiber 4 g
Sugar 8 g
Sodium 286 mg

151. Tomato Bulgur

Preparation Time: 7 minutes
Cooking Time: 20 minutes
Servings: 2
Ingredients:

- 1/2 cup bulgur
- 1 teaspoon tomato paste
- 1/2 white onion, diced
- 2 tablespoons coconut oil
- 1 1/2 cup chicken stock

Directions:

1. Set coconut oil in the pan and melt it. Attach diced onion and roast it until light brown. Then add bulgur and stir well. Cook bulgur in coconut oil for 3 minutes.
2. Then attach tomato paste and mix up bulgur until homogenous. Attach chicken stock. Close the lid and cook bulgur for 15 minutes over the medium heat.
3. The cooked bulgur should soak all liquid.

Nutrition:

Calories 257

Fat 14.5 g

Fiber 7.1 g

Carbs 30.2 g

Protein 5.2 g

152. Moroccan Style Couscous

Preparation Time: 10 minutes

Cooking Time: 10 minutes

Servings: 4

Ingredients:

- 1 cup yellow couscous
- 1/2 teaspoon ground cardamom
- 1 cup chicken stock
- 1 tablespoon butter
- 1 teaspoon salt
- 1/2 teaspoon red pepper

Directions:

1. Set butter in the pan and melt it. Attach couscous and roast it for 1 minute over the high heat. Then attach ground cardamom, salt, and red pepper.
2. Stir it well. Pour the chicken stock and bring the mixture to boil.
3. Set and simmer couscous for 5 minutes with the closed lid.

Nutrition:

Calories 196

Fat 3.4 g

Fiber 2.4 g

Carbs 35 g

Protein 5.9 g

153. Creamy Polenta

Preparation Time: 8 minutes

Cooking Time: 45 minutes

Servings: 4

Ingredients:

- 1 cup polenta
- 1 1/2 cup water
- 2 cups chicken stock
- 1/2 cup cream
- 1/3 cup Parmesan, grated

Directions:

1. Put polenta in the pot. Add water, chicken stock, cream, and Parmesan.
2. Mix up polenta well. Then preheat oven to 355F.
3. Cook polenta in the oven. Merge up the cooked meal with the help of the spoon carefully before serving.

Nutrition:

Calories 208

Fat 5.3 g

Fiber 1 g

Carbs 32.2

Protein 8 g

154. Mushroom Millet

Preparation Time: 10 minutes

Cooking Time: 15 minutes

Servings: 3

Ingredients:

- 1/4 cup mushrooms, sliced
- 3/4 cup onion, diced

- 1 tablespoon olive oil
- 1 teaspoon salt
- 3 tablespoons milk
- 1/2 cup millet
- 1 cup of water
- 1 teaspoon butter

Directions:

1. Set olive oil in the skillet then put the onion. Attach mushrooms and roast the vegetables for 10 minutes over the medium heat. Stir them from time to time.
2. Meanwhile, pour water in the pan. Add millet and salt. Cook the millet with the closed lid over the medium heat.
3. Then attach the cooked mushroom mixture in the millet. Add milk and butter. Mix up the millet well.

Nutrition:
Calories 198
Fat 7.7 g
Fiber 3.5 g
Carbs 27.9 g
Protein 4.7 g

155. Spicy Barley

Preparation Time: 7 minutes
Cooking Time: 42 minutes
Servings: 5
Ingredients:

- 1 cup barley
- 3 cups chicken stock
- 1/2 teaspoon cayenne pepper
- 1 teaspoon salt
- 1/2 teaspoon chili pepper
- 1/2 teaspoon ground black pepper
- 1 teaspoon butter
- 1 teaspoon olive oil

Directions:

1. Set barley and olive oil in the pan. Roast barley on high heat.
2. Stir it well. Then ttach salt, chili pepper, ground black pepper, cayenne pepper, and butter. Add chicken stock.
3. Secure the lid and cook barley for 40 minutes over the medium-low heat.

Nutrition:
Calories 152
Fat 2.9 g
Fiber 6.5 g
Carbs 27.8 g
Protein 5.1 g

156. Tender Farro

Preparation Time: 8 minutes
Cooking Time: 40 minutes
Servings: 4
Ingredients:

- 1 cup farro
- 3 cups beef broth
- 1 teaspoon salt
- 1 tablespoon almond butter
- 1 tablespoon dried dill

Directions:

1. Set farro in the pan. Add beef broth, dried dill, and salt.
2. Secure the lid and place the mixture to boil. Then boil it for 35 minutes over the medium-low heat. When the time is done, open the lid and add almond butter.
3. Mix up the cooked farro well.

Nutrition:
Calories 95
Fat 3.3 g
Fiber 1.3 g
Carbs 10.1 g
Protein 6.4 g

157. Wheatberry Salad

Preparation Time: 10 minutes
Cooking Time: 50 minutes
Servings: 2
Ingredients:

- 1/4 cup of wheat berries
- 1 cup of water
- 1 teaspoon salt
- 2 tablespoons walnuts, chopped
- 1 tablespoon chives, chopped
- 1/4 cup fresh parsley, chopped
- 2 oz. pomegranate seeds
- 1 tablespoon canola oil
- 1 teaspoon chili flakes

Directions:

1. Set wheat berries and water in the pan. Attach salt and simmer the ingredients for 50 minutes over the medium heat.
2. Meanwhile, merge up together walnuts, chives, parsley, pomegranate seeds, and chili flakes. When the wheatberry is cooked, et it in the walnut mixture.
3. Attach canola oil and mix up the salad well.

Nutrition:
Calories 160
Fat 11.8 g
Fiber 1.2 g
Carbs 12 g
Protein 3.4 g

158. Curry Wheatberry Rice

Preparation Time: 10 minutes
Cooking Time: 1 hour 15 minutes
Servings: 5
Ingredients:

- 1 tablespoon curry paste
- 1/4 cup milk
- 1 cup wheat berries
- 1/2 cup of rice
- 1 teaspoon salt
- 4 tablespoons olive oil
- 6 cups chicken stock

Directions:

1. Place wheat berries and chicken stock in the pan. Secure the lid and cook the mixture for 1 hour over the medium heat. Then add rice, olive oil, and salt.
2. Stir well. Mix up together milk and curry paste. Attach the curry liquid in the rice-wheatberry mixture and stir well. Set the meal for 15 minutes with the closed lid.
3. When the rice is processed, all the meal is cooked.

Nutrition:
Calories 232
Fat 15 g
Fiber 1.4 g
Carbs 23.5 g
Protein 3.9 g

159. Couscous Salad

Preparation Time: 10 minutes
Cooking Time: 6 minutes
Servings: 4
Ingredients:

- 1/3 cup couscous
- 1/3 cup chicken stock
- 1/4 teaspoon ground black pepper
- 3/4 teaspoon ground coriander
- 1/2 teaspoon salt

- 1/4 teaspoon paprika
- 1/4 teaspoon turmeric
- 1 tablespoon butter
- 2 oz. chickpeas, canned, drained
- 1 cup fresh arugula, chopped
- 2 oz. sun-dried tomatoes, chopped
- 1 oz. Feta cheese, crumbled
- 1 tablespoon canola oil

Directions:

1. Bring the chicken stock to boil. Attach couscous, ground black pepper, ground coriander, salt, paprika, and turmeric. Attach chickpeas and butter. Set the mixture well and close the lid.
2. Meanwhile, in the bowl combine together arugula, sun-dried tomatoes, and Feta cheese. Add cooked couscous mixture and canola oil.
3. Mix up the salad well.

Nutrition:

Calories 18

Fat 9 g

Fiber 3.6 g

Carbs 21.1 g

Protein 6 g

160. Farro Salad with Arugula

Preparation Time: 10 minutes

Cooking Time: 35 minutes

Servings: 2

Ingredients:

- 1/2 cup farro
- 1 1/2 cup chicken stock
- 1 teaspoon salt
- 1/2 teaspoon ground black pepper
- 2 cups arugula, chopped
- 1 cucumber, chopped
- 1 tablespoon lemon juice
- 1/2 teaspoon olive oil
- 1/2 teaspoon Italian seasoning

Directions:

1. Mrge up together farro, salt, and chicken stock and transfer mixture in the pan. Secure the lid and boil it for 35 minutes.
2. Meanwhile, set all remaining ingredients in the salad bowl. Chill the farro and add it in the salad bowl too.
3. Mix up the salad well.

Nutrition:

Calories 92

Fat 2.3 g

Fiber 2 g

Carbs 15.6 g

Protein 3.9 g

161. Cauliflower Broccoli Mash

Preparation Time: 5 minutes

Cooking Time: 10 minutes

Serving: 6

Ingredients:

- 1 large head cauliflower, cut into chunks
- 1 small head broccoli, cut into florets
- 3 tablespoons extra virgin olive oil
- 1 teaspoon salt
- Pepper, to taste

Directions:

1. Set a pot and add oil then heat it. Add the cauliflower and broccoli. Flavor with salt and pepper to taste. Keep stirring.
2. Add water if needed. When is already cooked, use a food processor or a potato masher to puree the vegetables. Serve and enjoy!

Nutrition:

Calories: 39

Fat: 3 g
Carbohydrates: 2 g
Protein: 0.89 g

162. Broccoli and Black Beans Stir Fry

Preparation Time: 10 minutes
Cooking Time: 15 minutes
Servings: 4
Ingredients:

- 4 cups broccoli florets
- 1 tablespoon sesame oil
- 4 teaspoons sesame seeds
- 2 teaspoons ginger, finely chopped
- A pinch turmeric powder
- Lime juice to taste (optional)
- 2 cups cooked black beans
- 2 cloves garlic, finely minced
- A large pinch red chili flakes
- Salt to taste

Directions:

1. Set enough water to cover the bottom of the saucepan by an inch. Place a strainer on the saucepan. Place broccoli florets on the strainer. Steam the broccoli for 6 minutes. Set a large frying pan over medium heat. Add sesame oil.
2. When the oil is warm, attach sesame seeds, chili flakes, ginger, garlic, turmeric powder and salt. Sauté. Attach steamed broccoli and black beans and sauté until thoroughly heated. Add lime juice and stir. Serve hot.

Nutrition:
Calories: 196 kcal
Protein: 11.2 g
Fat: 7.25 g
Carbohydrates: 23.45 g

163. Roasted Curried Cauliflower

Preparation Time: 5 minutes
Cooking Time: 30 minutes
Servings: 4
Ingredients:

- 1 large head cauliflower, cut into florets
- 1 tsp. curry powder
- 1 1/2 tbsp. olive oil
- 1 tsp. cumin seeds
- 1 tsp. mustard seeds
- 3/4 tsp. salt

Directions:

1. Preheat your oven to 375°F
2. Grease a baking sheet with cooking spray
3. Take a bowl and place all ingredients
4. Toss to coat well
5. Arrange the vegetable on a baking sheet
6. Roast for 30 minutes
7. Serve and enjoy!

Nutrition:
Calories: 67
Fat: 6 g
Carbs: 4 g
Protein: 2 g

164. Caramelized Pears and Onions

Preparation Time: 5 minutes
Cooking Time: 35 minutes
Servings: 4
Ingredients:

- 2 red onion, cut into wedges
- 2 firm red pears, cored and quartered
- 1 tbsp. olive oil
- Salt and pepper, to taste

Directions:

1. Preheat your oven to 425F
2. Set the pears and onion on a baking tray
3. Drizzle with olive oil
4. Season with salt and pepper
5. Bake in the oven for 35 minutes
6. Serve and enjoy!

Nutrition:
Calories: 101
Fat: 4 g
Carbs: 17 g
Protein: 1 g

165. Spicy Roasted Brussels Sprouts

Preparation Time: 5 minutes
Cooking Time: 30 minutes
Servings: 4
Ingredients:

- 1 1/4 pound Brussels sprouts, cut into florets
- 1/2 cup kimchi with juice
- 2 tbsps. olive oil
- Salt and pepper, to taste

Directions:

1. Set the oven to 425F.
2. Set the Brussels sprouts with pepper, salt, and oil.
3. Bake in the oven for 25 minutes
4. Detach from oven and mix with kimchi . Return to the oven. Cook for 5 minutes
5. Serve and enjoy!

Nutrition:
Calories: 135
Fat: 7 g
Carbs: 16 g
Protein: 5 g

166. Apple Sauce Treat

Preparation Time: 10 minutes
Cooking Time: 0 minutes
Servings: 1
Ingredients:

- 1/4 cup low-fat cottage cheese
- 1/4 cup unsweetened applesauce
- 1/2 tsp. cinnamon
- 1 1/2 tsp. toasted slivered almonds

Directions:

1. Merge the cottage cheese and applesauce in a bowl, stirring well.
2. Sprinkle with cinnamon and mix well.
3. Set the top with almonds, pick up your spoon, and enjoy.

Nutrition:
Calories: 225
Protein: 16.24 g
Fat: 14.17 g
Carbs: 8.54 g

167. Brownies Avocado

Preparation Time: 10 minutes
Cooking Time: 25 minutes
Servings: 6-8
Ingredients:

- 1/2 cup almond meal
- 3/4 cup cocoa powder
- 1 1/2 tsp. instant coffee

- 1/2 tsp. salt
- 2 cups nuts, chopped
- 1 avocado
- 1 apple
- 1 cup sweet potato
- 4 tbsps. ground chia seeds
- 1 tsp. vanilla
- 1/2 cup almond butter
- 1/2 cup coconut butter, softened
- 1/4 cup coconut oil
- 2 1/4 cup stevia

Directions:

1. Warmth the oven to 350F then line a 9 by 13-inch pan with parchment.
2. In a bowl, erge the almond meal, cocoa, coffee, cinnamon, salt, and nuts. Whisk and set aside.
3. Set the rest of the ingredients in a food processor and mix until smooth. Add the ingredients to the bowl and pulse. This combination should be chunky.
4. Set into pan and bake for at least 25 minutes.
5. Let cool and chill before slicing.

Nutrition:

Calories: 591

Protein: 11.03 g

Fat: 53.8 g

Carbs: 26.58 g

168. Brussels Sprout Chips

Preparation Time: 10 minutes

Cooking Time: 10 minutes

Servings: 4

Ingredients:

- 2 cups Brussels sprout leaves
- 2 tbsps. ghee
- Kosher salt
- 1 Lemon zest

Directions:

1. Warmth the oven to 350F, then cover two cookie sheets with parchment paper.
2. Put the leaves in a big bowl and pour melted ghee over the top, and add salt.
3. Bake until the leaves are crispy.
4. While still hot, set the lemon zest over the leaves. Serve warm.

Nutrition:

Calories: 42

Protein: 3.13 g

Fat: 1.68 g

Carbs: 4.77 g

169. Cauliflower Snacks

Preparation Time: 10 minutes

Cooking Time: 60 minutes

Servings: 4

Ingredients:

- 1 cauliflower head
- 4 tbsps. extra virgin olive oil
- 1 tsp. salt

Directions:

1. Warmth the oven to 425F, then prepare two cookie sheets by lining them with parchment paper.
2. Set off the cauliflower florets and discard the core. Cut the florets into golf-ball-sized pieces.
3. Set the cauliflower in a bowl and pour olive oil over them and sprinkle with salt. Mix to coat. Spread in a single layer, not touching.
4. Roast about 1 hour until golden brown. Serve warm.

Nutrition:

Calories: 91

Protein: 2.93 g

Fat: 7.7 g

Carbs: 3.29 g

170. Ginger Flour Banana Ginger Bars

Preparation Time: 10 minutes
Cooking Time: 40 minutes
Servings: 4-6
Ingredients:

- 1 cup coconut flour
- 1 1/2 tbsp. grated ginger
- 2 large ripe bananas
- 1 tsp. baking soda
- 1/3 cup melted butter
- 2 tsp. cinnamon
- 2 tsp. apple cider vinegar
- 1/3 cup honey or maple syrup
- 1 tsp. ground cardamom
- 6 medium while eggs

Directions:

1. Preheat the oven to 350F.
2. Set a glass baking dish with parchment paper
3. Set all the ingredients except the baking soda and apple cider vinegar through a food processor and blend until it's all mixed up.
4. Now attach the last two ingredients and blitz once before pouring the mix into the glass dish.
5. Bake and serve.

Nutrition:
Calories: 1407
Protein: 42.18 g
Fat: 100.26 g
Carbs: 88.33 g

171. Tangy Turmeric Flavored Florets

Preparation Time: 10 minutes
Cooking Time: 55 minutes
Servings: 1
Ingredients:

- 1 cauliflower head, chopped into florets
- 1 tbsp. olive oil
- 1 tbsp. turmeric
- A pinch of cumin
- A dash of salt

Directions:

1. Set the oven to 400F.
2. Set all the ingredients in a baking pan. Mix well until thoroughly combined.
3. Secure the pan with foil. Roast for 40 minutes. Remove the foil cover and roast additionally for 15 minutes.

Nutrition:
Calories: 90
Fat: 3 g
Protein: 4.5 g
Sodium: 87 mg
Total carbs: 16.2 g
Dietary Fiber: 5 g
Net Carbs: 11.2 g

172. Cool Garbanzo and Spinach Beans

Preparation Time: 5-10 minutes
Cooking Time: 5 minutes
Servings: 4
Ingredients:

- 12 oz. garbanzo beans
- 1 tbsp. olive oil
- 1/2 onion, diced
- 1/2 tsp. cumin
- 10 oz. spinach, chopped

Directions:

1. Set a skillet and add olive oil.
2. Set it over medium-low heat.
3. Attach onions, garbanzo and cook for 5 minutes.
4. Set in cumin, garbanzo beans, spinach, and season with sunflower seeds.
5. Use a spoon to smash gently.
6. Cook thoroughly.
7. Serve and enjoy!

Nutrition:
Calories: 90
Fat: 4 g
Carbs: 11 g
Protein: 4 g

173. Onion and Orange Healthy Salad

Preparation Time: 10 minutes
Cooking Time: 0 minutes
Servings: 3
Ingredients:

- 6 large oranges
- 3 tbsps. red wine vinegar
- 6 tbsps. olive oil
- 1 tsp. dried oregano
- 1 red onion, thinly sliced
- 1 cup olive oil
- 1/4 cup fresh chives, chopped
- Ground black pepper

Directions:

1. Set the orange and cut each of them into 4-5 crosswise slices.
2. Set the oranges to a shallow dish.
3. Whisk the vinegar, olive oil, and sprinkle oregano. Toss.
4. Set sliced onion and black olives on top.
5. Serve and enjoy!

Nutrition:
Calories: 120
Fat: 6 g
Carbs: 20 g
Protein: 2 g

174. Oven Crisp Sweet Potato

Preparation Time: 10 minutes
Cooking Time: 20 minutes
Servings: 2
Ingredients:

- 1 medium-sized sweet potato, raw
- 1 tsp. sugar
- 1 tsp. coconut oil

Directions:

1. Preheat the oven to 160C.
2. Divide the sweet potato into thin chips or strips. Wash and pat dry.
3. Drizzle the coconut oil over the potatoes. Toss until all chips are coated.
4. Set in an oven baking sheet. Bake for 10 minutes.
5. Take out the crispy sweet potatoes. Sprinkle with sugar and serve.

Nutrition:
Calories: 123
Protein: 4.23 g
Fat: 5.39 g
Carbs: 14.63 g

175. Olive and Tomato Balls

Preparation Time: 10 minutes
Cooking Time: 35 minutes
Servings: 5
Ingredients:

- 5 tbsps. parmesan cheese, grated
- 1/4 tsp. salt
- black pepper (as desired)
- 2 garlic cloves, crushed
- 4 kalamata olives, pitted
- 4 pcs. sun-dried tomatoes, drained
- 2 tbsps. oregano, chopped
- 2 tbsps. thyme, chopped
- 2 tbsps. basil, chopped
- 1/4 cup coconut oil
- 1/2 cup cream cheese

Directions:

1. Slice the coconut oil, attach it to a small mixing bowl with the cream cheese, and leave them to soften for about 30 minutes. Smash together and mix well to combine.
2. Attach in the Kalamata olives and sun-dried tomatoes and mix well before adding in the herbs and seasonings. Merge thoroughly before placing the mixing bowl in the refrigerator to allow the results to solidify.
3. Once it has solidified, set the mixture into a total of 5 balls using an ice cream scoop. Set each of the finished balls into the parmesan cheese before plating.
4. Store the extra's in the fridge in an air-tight container for up to 7 days.

Nutrition:
Calories: 212
Protein: 4.77 g
Fat: 20.75 g
Carbs: 3.13 g

Chapter 7. Desserts

176. Toasted Almond Ambrosia

Preparation Time: 10 minutes
Cooking Time: 60 minutes
Servings: 4
Ingredients:

- 1/2 cup sliced almonds
- 1/2 cup unsweetened grated coconut
- 1 small pineapple, diced (approximately 3 cups)
- 5 oranges, in segments
- 2 red apples, heartless and diced
- 1 peeled banana, cut lengthwise in half and sliced transversely
- 2 tablespoons Sherry Cream wine
- Fresh mint leaves to decorate

Directions:

1. Warmth the oven to 325 F (160 C). Place the almonds on a baking sheet and bake; Stir a few times until golden brown and give off its aroma, for about 10 minutes.
2. Transfer immediately to a plate to cool. Add the coconut to the tray and bake, frequently stirring, until lightly browned, for about 10 minutes.
3. Transfer immediately to a plate to cool.
4. In a large bowl, mix the pineapple, oranges, apples, banana, and sherry. Stir gently to mix well.
5. Place the fruit mixture evenly in different individual bowls. Sprinkle evenly with roasted almonds and coconut, then garnish with mint. Serve immediately.

Nutrition
Calories: 177
Total Fat: 5 g
Saturated Fat: 1 g
Cholesterol: 0mg
Sodium: 2mg
Total carbohydrate: 30 g
Dietary fiber: 6 g
Total sugars: 21 g
Protein: 3 g

177. Apricot Biscotti

Preparation Time: 10 minutes
Cooking Time: 40 minutes
Servings: 4-6
Ingredients:

- 3/4 cup bran flour (whole wheat)
- 3/4 cup common flour (white)
- 1/4 cup brown sugar, very compact
- 1 teaspoon baking powder
- 2 eggs, lightly beaten
- 2 tablespoons 1 percent low-fat milk
- 2 tablespoons canola oil
- 2 tablespoons dark honey
- 1/2 teaspoon almond extract
- 2/3 cup chopped dried apricots
- 1/4 cup large chopped almonds

Directions:

1. Warmth the oven to 350 F (175 C).
2. In a large bowl, place the flour, brown sugar and baking powder.
3. Beat until mixed. Add eggs, milk, canola oil, honey, and almond extract.
4. Set with a wooden spoon until the dough begins to integrate. Add almonds and chopped

apricots. With floured hands, mix the dough until the ingredients are well integrated.

5. Place the dough on a large sheet of plastic wrap and form a crushed roll 12 inches (30 cm) long, 3 inches (7.5 cm) wide and about 1 inch (2.5 cm) by hand.

6. High Lift the plastic wrap and invert the dough in a non-stick baking sheet. Bake for 25-30 minutes, until lightly browned.

7. Transfer it to another baking sheet and let it cool for 10 minutes. Leave the oven at 350 F (175 C).

8. Place the cold dough on a cutting board. With a serrated knife, cut transversely into 24 1/2 inch (1 cm) wide portions. Place the portions with the cut down on the baking sheet.

9. Bake again for 15-20 minutes, until crispy. Go to a rack and let cool completely.

10. Store in an airtight container.

Nutrition

Calories: 75

Total Fat: 2 g

Cholesterol: 15mg

Sodium: 17mg

Total carbohydrate: 12 g

Dietary fiber: 1 g

Total sugars: 6 g

Added sugars: 2 g

Protein: 2 g

178. Apple and Berry Cobbler

Preparation Time: 10 minutes

Cooking Time: 20 minutes

Servings: 2

Ingredients:

- 1 cup fresh raspberries
- 1 cup fresh blueberries
- 2 cups chopped apples
- 2 tablespoons turbinado sugar or brown sugar
- 1/2 teaspoon ground cinnamon
- 1 teaspoon lemon zest
- 2 teaspoons lemon juice
- 1 1/2 tablespoon cornstarch

For the coating:

- 1 large egg white
- 1/4 cup soy milk
- 1/4 teaspoon salt
- 1/2 teaspoon of vanilla
- 1 1/2 tablespoon of turbinado sugar or brown sugar
- 3/4 cup pastry whole meal flour

Directions:

1. Warmth the oven to 350 F (175 C). Lightly cover 6 individual baking pans with oil spray.

2. In a bowl, attach the raspberries, blueberries, apples, sugar, cinnamon, lemon zest, and lemon juice. Stir to mix well. Add the cornstarch and stir until dissolved.

3. In a bowl, attach the egg white and beat until lightly beaten. Add soy milk, salt, vanilla, sugar, and baking flour. Stir to mix well.

4. Divide the berry mixture evenly between the prepared dishes. Pour the mixture over each dish. Organize the casseroles in a large baking dish and place it in the oven.

5. Bake the berries until they are tender and the topping is golden brown, about 30 minutes. Serve warm.

Nutrition

Calories: 136

Trans Fat: 0 g

Cholesterol: 0mg

Sodium: 111mg

Total carbohydrate: 31 g

Dietary fiber: 4 g

Added sugars: 7 g

Protein: 3 g

179. Chocolate Mascarpone

Preparation Time: 10 minutes
Cooking Time: 40 minutes
Servings: 4-6
Ingredients:

- 250ml. fondant cream (well chilled)
- 250g. Mascarpone cheese
- 200 g. Dark chocolate
- 4 tablespoons powdered sugar

Directions:

1. Applying cream, we dissolve chocolate in a water bath - i.e., place the chocolate in a glass bowl. Set the bowl on a pot with boiling water - so that the bottom of the bowl does not touch the water.
2. Leave the melted chocolate to cool (until it is not hot, only slightly warm). Whip cream.
3. Mix mascarpone cheese with a mixer with powdered sugar. Without stopping the mixer - we add chocolate to the cheese (gently pour in a small stream). Mix until smooth.
4. Add whipped cream to the chocolate mass. Then mix - manually or with a mixer at low speed until we get a uniform, creamy, thick consistency.
5. To get a nice-looking dessert - apply the cream to the cup using the sleeve to decorate the cakes.
6. We store the ready cream in the fridge.

Nutrition:
Calories: 591
Protein: 11.03 g
Fat: 53.8 g
Carbs: 26.58 g

180. Almond Ricotta Spread

Preparation Time: 10 minutes
Cooking Time: 35 minutes
Servings: 5
Ingredients:

- 200 gr. raw and unsalted almonds
- 100 gr. raw and unsalted cashews
- 2 tablespoons lemon juice
- Sea salt at ease
- 1 tablespoon of yeast in "Titan"
- Black pepper to taste
- Fresh herbs to taste (rosemary, parsley, dill, sage, thyme, coriander)

Directions

1. Soak the nuts.
2. The next day, strain the nuts and process them with lemon juice, salt, flaked yeast (or very fine grated "Viol life" cheese) and pepper until a thick cream is formed.
3. Turn the processor on and off if necessary, and stir well so that everything is well integrated.
4. Some water can be added, but not in excess to prevent the dip from becoming too liquid. It should have the consistency of the traditional "pillory."
5. Rectify the salt and pepper again and add fresh herbs on top.

Nutrition:
Calories: 591
Protein: 11.03 g
Fat: 53.8 g
Carbs: 26.58 g

181. Baklava with Lemon Honey Syrup

Preparation Time: 10 minutes
Cooking Time: 0 minutes
Servings: 3
Ingredients:

- 400g of filo pastry
- 300g of walnuts
- 250g of pistachios
- 200g of butter
- 200g of sugar
- a tablespoon of lemon juice
- 2 tablespoons of honey
- 300 ml of water

Directions:

1. Melt the butter in a saucepan and let it cool, while chopping the pistachios and almonds together with two tablespoons of sugar.
2. Butter the pan, then spread the first sheet of phyllo dough, brush it with the melted butter and place a second and a third on it, still buttering.
3. After the third layer, place chopped walnuts and pistachios and start the process again: for every 3 sheets of buttered pasta, insert a layer of walnuts and pistachios until you finish with the filo pastry.
4. Bake at 180 for 15 minutes. Meanwhile, prepare the syrup, bring to a boil (over medium heat and stir constantly) the sugar, water, lemon juice, and honey.
5. Once cooked sprinkle the syrup baklava, let it cool and serve cut into diamonds and covered with chopped walnuts and pistachios.

Nutrition:
Calories: 591
Protein: 11.03 g
Fat: 53.8 g
Carbs: 26.58 g

182. Kourabiedes Greek Butter Cookies

Preparation Time: 5-10 minutes
Cooking Time: 5 minutes
Servings: 4
Ingredients:

- 150g raw almonds
- 155g soft butter (at room temperature)
- 70g caster sugar
- 2 egg yolks
- 300g flour 00
- 1/2 teaspoon baking powder
- Icing sugar to taste
- 20 whole cloves

Directions:

1. Bring a saucepan to boil with water. When the water boils, add the almonds, cook for 10 minutes and then drain on a sheet of absorbent paper. Remove the almond skin.
2. Light the oven at 200 C, cover a baking sheet with baking paper and toast the almonds. When they are well toasted, let them cool. Once cold, whisk it with a chopper. Do not reduce them to flour, but get a fine grain.
3. Whip the butter with the sugar, helping yourself with the electric whisk until you get froth. Add the egg yolks and mix with the whisk until all the ingredients are mixed. Sift the flour and baking powder.
4. Attach the flour, baking powder and chopped almonds to the dough. Start kneading in the bowl, then move to a table and knead: it takes a little patience before the dough becomes compact. As soon as you get compact dough, wrap it in plastic wrap and let it rest in the fridge for an hour.
5. As soon as this time has elapsed, preheat the oven to 180 ° C and cover a baking sheet with baking paper. Set balls about the size of a walnut and place them on the baking tray, placing them at a distance of two cm from each other.

6. Press the center of each ball with the fingertips, so as to obtain a small furrow and until golden brown. When baked, put a clove in the center of each cookie.
7. Let them cool and then sprinkle with plenty of icing sugar.

Nutrition:
Calories: 42
Protein: 3.13 g
Fat: 1.68 g
Carbs: 4.77 g

183. Cocoa Muffins with Coffee

Preparation Time: 10 minutes
Cooking Time: 20 minutes
Servings: 2
Ingredients:

- 1/2 hour soft butter
- 1 egg
- 1 teaspoon sugar
- 1 teaspoon vanilla
- 1 -1/2 teaspoon flour
- 1 teaspoon baking soda
- salt
- 1/2 teaspoon cocoa
- 1/2 teaspoon yogurt
- 1/3 teaspoon strong coffee

Directions:

1. Beat the butter with the sugar, add the egg and vanilla.
2. Mix flour, baking soda, salt, cocoa separately.
3. Add the dry ingredients of the parts together with the yogurt and the coffee parts to the egg mixture.
4. Warmth the oven to 180 degrees, fill the muffin cups with 2/3 of the mixture and bake for 20-25 minutes. or until ready.
5. For the glaze, I experimented and made it with liquid pastry cream / about 3/4 cup of tea / and a packet of 1 kg powdered sugar (I didn't get the whole packet). The mixture should be thick.

Nutrition:
Calories 95
Fat 3.3 g
Fiber 1.3 g
Carbs 10.1 g
Protein 6.4 g

184. Pumpkin Cupcake for Halloween

Preparation Time: 10 minutes
Cooking Time: 20 minutes
Servings: 2
Ingredients:

- products for your favorite cupcake
- products for your favorite cake
- cream pastry cream
- orange pastry
- round cupcake with a hole

Directions:

1. Bake two cupcakes according to your favorite recipe in a round shape with a hole. Allow them to cool in shape and then flip them over to remove them. Cut the bottom of the cupcakes - where they came up when baking - to make them even. Save the clippings.
2. Grease the flat side of one of the cupcakes with your favorite cake cream and blend in with the other.
3. Fill the hole in the middle with the cream-mixed cuts. Spread the pumpkin with the pastry cream outside.

4. Whisk the pastry cream with the mixer until thick and smooth. Paint it with orange pastry paint. Apply the pumpkin - it is already orange.
5. Pour a little of the cream to fill the gap in the middle. Make a "handle" from a celery stalk, or a twig, or whatever you have on hand.

Nutrition:
Calories: 216
Protein: 8.83 g
Fat: 11.48 g
Carbs: 21.86 g

185. Low Carb Nougat Whims

Preparation Time: 10 minutes
Cooking Time: 40 minutes
Servings: 4-6
Ingredients:

- 210g dark chocolate with a minimum of 70% cocoa solids
- 125 ml (110 g) coconut oil, divided
- 400g coconut milk, only the solid part
- 8 tbsp. peanut butter or other nut butter you like
- 1 tbsp. (5 g) cocoa powder
- 1 tsp. vanilla extract

Directions:
1. Dissolve half of the chocolate in a water bath or microwave over low heat. Add a quarter of coconut oil and mix well.
2. Pour into a greased mold and coated with baking paper (approximately 13 x 20 inches, if you make 40) and let cool in the refrigerator or freezer.
3. Carefully heat the solid part of the coconut milk (canned) in a different pan. Let it simmer for a few minutes.
4. Add half of the coconut oil, nut butter, cocoa powder, and vanilla while stirring. Make a smooth mixture. If the dough separates, use a hand blender and press several times to make it uniform.
5. Detach from heat and pour over chocolate. Set the pan to the refrigerator or freezer to cool again while the rest of the chocolate melts as in step 1.
6. Attach the remaining coconut oil to the chocolate and mix. Spread it in a layer over the cold nougat. Replace in the refrigerator and let stand for at least an hour, preferably longer.
7. Cut into 30-40 small pieces. Set in an airtight container in the refrigerator or freezer. The nougat is best served slightly cold.

Nutrition:
Calories: 288
Fat: 12g
Sat Fat: 1g
Carbohydrates: 41g
Fiber: 5g
Protein: 6g
Sodium: 125mg

186. Raspberry Feast Meringue with Cream Diplomat

Preparation Time: 10 minutes
Cooking Time: 60 minutes
Servings: 4
Ingredients:

- 2 egg whites
- 1/2 cup caster sugar
- 1/4 tsp. vanilla extract
- 1/4 cup crumbled barley sugar
- 1 cup frozen raspberries
- 1/4 cup water
- 2 tbsp. Raspberry Jell-O Powder with No Added Sugar
- 1 1/2 cup Cool Whip
- 1 bowl fresh raspberries

Directions:
1. To make the meringue, preheat the oven to 350 F (175 C) and line a baking sheet with parchment paper.
2. In a blender or bowl, whisk egg whites until the foam is obtained. Gently add the sugar while

whisking until you get firm, shiny picks. Stir in vanilla extract and crumbled barley sugar.

3. Shape the meringues on the coated cookie sheet and place in the preheated oven. Turn off the oven and wait 2 hours. Do not open the oven. Once the meringues are dry, break the meringues into small bites.

4. To make the mousse, put frozen raspberries and water in a small saucepan. Heat until raspberries melt and are tender. Put these raspberries in a blender. Add the Jell-O powder and mix. Once the raspberries have completely cooled, incorporate the Cool Whip.

5. To shape the raspberry, place in balloon glasses for individual portions or in a large cake pan first a layer of raspberry mousse, then a layer of meringue, then fresh raspberries. Repeat the layers. Refrigerate for a few hours before serving.

Nutrition:

Calories: 99 kcal

Fat: 4 g

Protein: 1 g

Sodium: 1,348 mg

Fiber: 4 g

Carbohydrates: 16 g

Sugar: 7 g

187. Cheesecake Mousse with Raspberries

Preparation Time: 10 minutes

Cooking Time: 40 minutes

Servings: 4-6

Ingredients:

- 1 cup light lemonade filling
- 1 can 8 oz. cream cheese at room temperature
- 3/4 cup SPLENDA no-calorie sweetener pellets
- 1 tbsp. at t. of lemon zest
- 1 tbsp. at t. vanilla extract
- 1 cup fresh or frozen raspberries

Directions

1. Beat the cream cheese until it is sparkling; add 1/2 cup SPLENDA Granules and mix until melted. Stir in lemon zest and vanilla.

2. Reserve some raspberries for decoration. Set the rest of the raspberries with a fork and mix them with 1/4 cup SPLENDA pellets until they are melted.

3. Lightly add the lump and cheese filling, and then gently but quickly add crushed raspberries. Share this mousse in 6 ramekins with a spoon and keep in the refrigerator until tasting.

4. Garnish mousses with reserved raspberries and garnish with fresh mint before serving.

Nutrition

Calories 734

Carbohydrates 37g

Cholesterol 115mg

Total Fat 54g

Protein 25g

188. Almond Meringue Cookies

Preparation Time: 10 minutes

Cooking Time: 30 minutes

Servings: 2

Ingredients

- 2 egg whites or 4 tbsp. pasteurized egg whites
- 1 Tbsp. tartar cream
- 1/2 tsp.
- 1/2 teaspoon almond extract vanilla extract
- 1/2 cup white sugar

Directions:

1. Preheat the oven to 300F.

2. Set the egg whites with the cream of tartar until the volume has doubled. Add other ingredients and whip until peaks form.

3. Using two teaspoons drop a spoonful of meringue onto parchment paper with the back of the other spoon.

4. Bake at 300F for about 25 minutes or until the meringues are crisp. Place in an airtight container.

Nutrition:
Calories 198
Fat 7.7 g
Fiber 3.5 g
Carbs 27.9 g
Protein 4.7 g
CHAPTER 12: SIDE DISH
94. Pesto Mushrooms
Preparation time: 40 minutes
Ingredients for 6 people

- pepper to taste
- 1 garlic clove
- 200 gr chestnut flour
- 1 glasses of extra virgin olive oil
- 240 gr flour
- 200 gr porcini mushrooms
- 3 tablespoons olive oil
- salt totaste
- 2 thyme sprig
- 4 eggs
- 1 glasses white wine
- 1 bunch of basil
- 1 bunch parsley

Preparation

1. Sifted to the fountain gr. 240 of white flour and gr. 200 of chestnut flour.
2. Add a pinch of salt, break 4 eggs in the center and beat them. Knead the dough until it becomes smooth and homogeneous.
3. Let it rest for 30 minutes, roll out the pastry and cut the noodles. Meanwhile, you cleaned gr. 200 fresh porcini mushrooms, slice them and sauté in a pan with a chopped clove of garlic, 2 sprigs of thyme and 3 tablespoons of oil.
4. Sprinkle the mushrooms with a small glass of white wine, let it evaporate, add salt and pepper and chop them in the mixer.
5. Prepare a pesto with a bunch of parsley, one of basil, 10 peeled almonds, salt, pepper and a small glass of extra virgin olive oil.
6. Mix the chopped herbs with the porcini mushrooms.
7. Cook the tagliatelle and season with the sauce.

189. Apple and Berries Ambrosia

Preparation time: 15 minutes
Cooking time: 0 minutes
Servings: 4
Ingredients:

- 2 cups unsweetened coconut milk, chilled
- 2 tablespoons raw honey
- 1 apple, peeled, cored, and chopped
- 2 cups fresh raspberries
- 2 cups fresh blueberries

Directions:

1. Set the chilled milk in a large bowl, then mix in the honey. Stir to mix well.
2. Then mix in the remaining ingredients. Stir to coat the fruits well and serve immediately.

Nutrition:
Calories: 386
Fat: 21.1g
Protein: 4.2g
Carbs: 45.9g

190. Banana, Cranberry, and Oat Bars

Preparation time: 15 minutes
Cooking time: 40 minutes
Servings: 16 bars
Ingredients:

- 2 tablespoon extra-virgin olive oil
- 2 medium ripe bananas, mashed
- 1/2 cup almond butter
- 1/2 cup maple syrup
- 1/3 cup dried cranberries
- 11/2 cups old-fashioned rolled oats
- 1/4 cup oat flour
- 1/4 cup ground flaxseed
- 1/4 teaspoon ground cloves
- 1/2 cup shredded coconut
- 1/2 teaspoon ground cinnamon
- 1 teaspoon vanilla extract

Directions:

1. Preheat the oven to 400F (205c). Set an 8-inch square pan with parchment paper, then grease with olive oil.
2. Combine the mashed bananas, almond butter, and maple syrup in a bowl. Stir to mix well. Merge in the remaining ingredients and stir to mix well until thick and sticky.
3. Spread the mixture evenly on the square pan with a spatula, then bake for 40 minutes or until a toothpick inserted in the center comes out clean.
4. Remove them from the oven and slice into 16 bars to serve.

Nutrition:
Calories: 145
Fat: 7.2g
Protein: 3.1g
Carbs: 18.9g

191. Berry and Rhubarb Cobbler

Preparation time: 15 minutes
Cooking time: 35 minutes
Servings: 8
Ingredients:
Cobbler:

- 1 cup fresh raspberries
- 2 cups fresh blueberries
- 1 cup sliced (1/2-inch) rhubarb pieces
- 1 tablespoon arrowroot powder
- 1/4 cup unsweetened apple juice
- 2 tablespoons melted coconut oil
- 1/4 cup raw honey

Topping:

- 1 cup almond flour
- 1 tablespoon arrowroot powder
- 1/2 cup shredded coconut
- 1/4 cup raw honey
- 1/2 cup coconut oil

Directions:

1. Preheat the oven to 350F (180c). Set a baking dish with melted coconut oil. Combine the ingredients for the cobbler in a large bowl. Stir to mix well. Spread the mixture in the single layer on the baking dish. Set aside.
2. Combine the almond flour, arrowroot powder, and coconut in a bowl. Stir to mix well. Fold in the honey and coconut oil. Stir with a fork until the mixture crumbled.
3. Spread the topping over the cobbler, then bake in the preheated oven for 35 minutes or until frothy and golden brown. Serve immediately.

Nutrition:
Calories: 305
Fat: 22.1g
Protein: 3.2g
Carbs: 29.8g

192. Citrus Cranberry and Quinoa Energy Bites

Preparation time: 15 minutes
Cooking time: 0 minutes
Servings: 12 bites
Ingredients:

- 2 tablespoons almond butter
- 2 tablespoons maple syrup
- 3/4 cup cooked quinoa
- 1 tablespoon dried cranberries
- 1 tablespoon chia seeds
- 1/4 cup ground almonds
- 1/4 cup sesame seeds, toasted
- Zest of 1 orange
- 1/2 teaspoon vanilla extract

Directions:

1. Line a baking sheet with parchment paper. Merge the butter and maple syrup in a bowl. Stir to mix well.
2. Fold in the remaining ingredients and stir until the mixture holds together and smooth. Set the mixture into 12 equal parts, then shape each part into a ball.
3. Arrange the balls on the baking sheet, then refrigerate for at least 15 minutes. Serve chilled.

Nutrition:
Calories: 110
Fat: 10.8g
Protein: 3.1g
Carbs: 4.9g

193. Chocolate, Almond, and Cherry Clusters

Preparation time: 15 minutes
Cooking time: 3 minutes
Servings: 10 clusters
Ingredients:

- 1 cup dark chocolate (60% cocoa or higher), chopped
- 1 tablespoon coconut oil
- 1/2 cup dried cherries
- 1 cup roasted salted almonds

Directions:

1. Line a baking sheet with parchment paper. Dissolve the chocolate and coconut oil in a saucepan for 3 minutes. Stir constantly.
2. Turn off the heat and mix in the cherries and almonds. Drop the mixture on the baking sheet with a spoon. Place the sheet in the refrigerator and chill for at least 1 hour or until firm. Serve chilled.

Nutrition:
Calories: 197
Fat: 13.2g
Protein: 4.1g
Carbs: 17.8g

194. Chocolate and Avocado Mousse

Preparation time: 15 minutes
Cooking time: 5 minutes
Servings: 4-6
Ingredients:

- 8 ounces (227 g) dark chocolate (60% cocoa or higher), chopped
- 1/4 cup unsweetened coconut milk
- 2 tablespoons coconut oil
- 2 ripe avocados, deseeded
- 1/4 cup raw honey
- Sea salt, to taste

Directions:

1. Put the chocolate in a saucepan. Set in the coconut milk and add the coconut oil. Cook for 3 minutes or until the chocolate and coconut oil melt. Stir constantly.
2. Put the avocado in a food processor, then drizzle with honey and melted chocolate. Pulse to combine until smooth.
3. Pour the mixture in a serving bowl, then sprinkle with salt. Refrigerate to chill for 30 minutes and serve.

Nutrition:
Calories: 654
Fat: 46.8g
Protein: 7.2g
Carbs: 55.9g

195. Coconut Blueberries with Brown Rice

Preparation time: 15 minutes
Cooking time: 10 minutes
Servings: 4
Ingredients:

- 1 cup fresh blueberries
- 2 cups unsweetened coconut milk
- 1 teaspoon ground ginger
- 1/4 cup maple syrup
- Sea salt, to taste
- 2 cups cooked brown rice

Directions:

1. Put all the ingredients, except for the brown rice, in a pot. Stir to combine well. Cook until the blueberries are tender.
2. Pour in the brown rice and cook for 3 more minute or until the rice is soft. Stir constantly. Serve immediately.

Nutrition:
Calories: 470
Fat: 24.8g
Protein: 6.2g
Carbs: 60.1g

196. Cucumber Sandwich Bites

Preparation Time: 5 minutes
Cooking Time: 0 minutes
Servings: 12
Ingredients:

- 1 cucumber, sliced
- 8 slices whole wheat bread
- 2 tablespoons cream cheese, soft
- 1 tablespoon chives, chopped
- 1/4 cup avocado
- 1 teaspoon mustard
- Salt and black pepper to the taste

Directions:

1. Set the mashed avocado on each bread slice, also spread the rest of the ingredients except the cucumber slices.
2. Set the cucumber slices on the bread slices, cut each slice in thirds, set on a platter and serve as an appetizer.

Nutrition:
Calories 187
Fat 12.4g
Carbohydrates 4.5g
Protein 8.2g

197. Yogurt Dip

Preparation Time: 10 minutes
Cooking Time: 0 minutes
Servings: 6
Ingredients:

- 2 cups Greek yogurt
- 2 tablespoons pistachios, toasted and chopped
- A pinch of salt and white pepper
- 2 tablespoons mint, chopped
- 1 tablespoon kalamata olives, pitted and chopped
- 1/4 cup zaatar spice
- 1/4 cup pomegranate seeds
- 1/3 cup olive oil

Directions:

1. Mix the yogurt with the pistachios and the rest of the ingredients, whisk well, set into small cups and serve with pita chips.

Nutrition:
Calories 294
Fat 18g
Carbohydrates 2g
Protein 10g

198. Olives and Cheese Stuffed Tomatoes

Preparation Time: 10 minutes
Cooking Time: 0 minutes
Servings: 24
Ingredients:

- 24 tomatoes
- 2 tablespoons olive oil
- 1/4 teaspoon red pepper flakes
- 1/2 cup feta cheese, crumbled
- 2 tablespoons black olive paste
- 1/4 cup mint

Directions:

1. In a bowl, merge the olives paste with the rest of the ingredients except the cherry tomatoes and whisk well. Stuff the cherry tomatoes with this mix, arrange them all on a platter and serve as an appetizer.

Nutrition:
Calories 136
Fat 8.6g
Carbohydrates 5.6g
Protein 5.1g

199. Pepper Tapenade

Preparation Time: 10 minutes
Cooking Time: 0 minutes
Servings: 4
Ingredients:

- 7 ounces roasted red peppers, chopped
- 1/2 cup parmesan, grated
- 1/3 cup parsley, chopped
- 14 ounces canned artichokes, drained and chopped
- 3 tablespoons olive oil
- 1/4 cup capers, drained
- 1 and 1/2 tablespoons lemon juice
- 2 garlic cloves, minced

Directions

1. In a blender, merge the red peppers with the parmesan and the rest of the ingredients and pulse well. Set into cups and serve as a snack.

Nutrition:
Calories 200
Fat 5.6g
Carbohydrates 12.4g
Protein 4.6g

200. Coriander Falafel

Preparation Time: 10 minutes
Cooking Time: 10 minutes
Servings: 8
Ingredients:

- 1 cup canned garbanzo beans
- 1 bunch parsley leaves
- 1 yellow onion, chopped
- 5 garlic cloves, minced
- 1 teaspoon coriander, ground
- A pinch of salt and black pepper
- 1/4 teaspoon cayenne pepper
- 1/4 teaspoon baking soda
- 1/4 teaspoon cumin powder
- 1 teaspoon lemon juice
- 3 tablespoons flour
- Olive oil

Directions

1. Merge the beans with the parsley, onion and the rest the ingredients except the oil and the flour and pulse well.
2. Set the mix to a bowl, attach the flour, stir well, shape 16 balls out of this mix and flatten them a bit.
3. Preheat pan over medium-high heat, add the falafels, cook them for 5 minutes on both sides, put in paper towels, drain excess grease, arrange them on a platter and serve as an appetizer.

Nutrition:
Calories 122
Fat 6.2g
Carbohydrates 12.3g
Protein 3.1g

Chapter 8. 6 Week Meal Plan

First Week

DAY	BREAKFAST	LUNCH	DINNER
DAY-1	Spinach Frittata	Grilled Avocado Sandwich	Chicken Bone Broth
DAY-2	Mushroom and Bell Pepper Omelet	Cauliflower Steaks with Tamarind and Beans	Chicken Bone Broth with Ginger and Lemon
DAY-3	Yogurt, Berry, and Walnut Parfait	Smoked Salmon Tartine	Vegetable Stock
DAY-4	Oatmeal and Cinnamon with Dried Cranberries	Healthy Chicken Marsala	Chicken Vegetable Soup
DAY-5	Green Tea and Ginger Shake	Grilled Salmon Burgers	Carrot Ginger Soup
DAY-6	Smoked Salmon Scrambled Eggs	Tuna Steaks	Turkey Sweet Potato Hash
DAY-7	Chia Breakfast Pudding	Air Fryer Salmon	Turkey Taco Lettuce Boats

Second Week

DAY	BREAKFAST	LUNCH	DINNER
DAY-1	Coconut Rice with Berries	Rosemary Garlic Lamb Chops	Turkey and Greens Meatloaf
DAY-2	Overnight Muesli	Mushroom Farro Risotto	Simple Italian Seasoned Turkey Breast
DAY-3	Spicy Quinoa	Instant Pot Black Beans	Spiced Chicken and Vegetables
DAY-4	Buckwheat Crêpes with Berries	Popcorn Chicken	Lemon Garlic Turkey Breast
DAY-5	Warm Chia-Berry Non-dairy Yogurt	Banana Bread	Home-style Chicken and Vegetables
DAY-6	Buckwheat Waffles	Pumpkin Protein Bowl	Chicken Tenders with Honey Mustard Sauce
DAY-7	Coconut Pancakes	Baked French Toast Casserole	Chicken Breasts with Cabbage and Mushrooms

Third Week

DAY	BREAKFAST	LUNCH	DINNER
DAY-1	Spinach Muffins	Whole Grain Blueberry Scones	Ground Turkey with Peas and Potato
DAY-2	Choco Chia Banana Bowl	Pan-Seared Scallops with Lemon-Ginger Vinaigrette	Turkey and Veggies Chili
DAY-3	Blueberry Breakfast Blend	Manhattan-Style Salmon Chowder	Roasted Whole Turkey
DAY-4	Quick Quinoa with Cinnamon and Chia	Sesame-Tuna Skewers	Duck with Bok Choy
DAY-5	Plum, Pear and Berry-Baked Brown Rice Recipe	Trout with Chard	Beef with Mushroom and Broccoli
DAY-6	Good Grains with Cranberries and Cinnamon	Seafood Noodles	Beef with Zucchini Noodles
DAY-7	Seared Syrupy Sage Pork Patties	Spicy Pulled Chicken Wraps	Spiced Ground Beef

Fourth Week

DAY	BREAKFAST	LUNCH	DINNER
DAY-1	Waffles Whipped With Perfect Plantain Pair	Apricot Chicken Wings	Ground Turkey with Peas and Potato
DAY-2	Turkey with Thyme and Sage Sausage	Champion Chicken Pockets	Turkey and Veggies Chili
DAY-3	Sweet and Savory Breakfast Hash	Chicken-Bell Pepper Sauté	Roasted Whole Turkey
DAY-4	Five-Minute Avocado Toast	Curried Beef Meatballs	Duck with Bok Choy
DAY-5	Healthy Chickpea Scramble Stuffed Sweet Potatoes	Beef Meatballs in Tomato Gravy	Beef with Mushroom and Broccoli
DAY-6	High-Protein: Breakfast Bowl	Pork with Lemongrass	Beef with Zucchini Noodles
DAY-7	Green Smoothie Bowl	Pork with Olives	Spiced Ground Beef

Fifth Week

DAY	VEGETABLES	SEAFOOD AND FISH	SIDE DISHES
DAY-1	Spicy Three Beans Chili	Almond Pesto Salmon	Green Beans
DAY-2	Chickpeas Chili	Baked Coconut Shrimp	Roasted Carrots
DAY-3	Lentils Chili	Broiled Dill Tilapia Parmesan	Tomato Bulgur
DAY-4	Grains Chili	Delicious Parmesan Shrimp	Moroccan Style Couscous
DAY-5	Red Lentils Curry	Lemon Butter Scallops	Creamy Polenta
DAY-6	Red Lentils with Spinach	Lemon Garlic Mahi-Mahi Fillets	Mushroom Millet
DAY-7	Vegetarian Balls in Gravy	Lemon Garlic Shrimp Pasta	Spicy Barley

Sixth Week

DAY	VEGETABLES	SEAFOOD AND FISH	SIDE DISHES
DAY-1	Quinoa with Veggies	Mediterranean Grilled Ahi Tuna	Tender Farro
DAY-2	Quinoa with Asparagus	Piccata Fish Cakes	Wheatberry Salad
DAY-3	Quinoa and Beans with Veggies	Salmon Cakes	Curry Wheatberry Rice
DAY-4	Coconut Brown Rice	Salmon with Spinach and Pesto	Couscous Salad
DAY-5	Brown Rice and Cherries Pilaf	Seafood Imperial	Farro Salad with Arugula
DAY-6	Brown Rice Casserole	Sesame Ginger Salmon	Stir-Fried Farros
DAY-7	Rice, Lentils and Veggie Casserole	Shrimp Alfredo	Cauliflower Broccoli Mash

Conclusion

So many people have trouble with chronic inflammation. This has been negatively affecting their health, including their weight, mood, and energy. This anti-inflammatory diet plan will help you avoid those effects. It focuses on small changes to your habits that lead to significant improvements in inflammation by helping your body fight infections and illness better. To follow the Anti-Inflammatory Diet, you will need to look at your diet and think about changing certain things to follow this new plan.

In addition, knowing what foods are best for you will help you make sure that you are eating right. The key to the Anti-Inflammatory Diet is to focus on eating more anti-inflammatory foods that will help your body fight off the inflammation. Perhaps you have been suffering from chronic pain but never knew what was causing it.

The diet listed above is not only healthy for your body, but it's also healthy for your mind and body. You'll have more energy, a sharper memory, and superb quality of life when you start eating this way. The anti-inflammatory diet promotes a healthy lifestyle with a simple change in what you eat that can benefit not only you but also those around you. Healing Diet is a term often used to describe the anti-inflammatory diet. Within the pages of this book, you will find information about what an Anti-Inflammatory Diet is, what it can do for your mind and body, how to make it work for you, who should follow this type of diet, and much more.

The anti-inflammatory diet aims to lower arachidonic acid consumption by eliminating meat from your diet entirely or limiting it significantly. This helps you decrease the presence of arachidonic acid in your body, making you less likely to suffer from inflammatory diseases.

Let us all find out more about what an anti-inflammatory diet is to get started on a path to healing.

.

Printed in Great Britain
by Amazon